WILLIAM BLAKE: BOOK ILLUSTRATOR

WILLIAM BLAKE: BOOK ILLUSTRATOR

A BIBLIOGRAPHY AND CATALOGUE OF THE COMMERCIAL ENGRAVINGS

BY

ROGER R. EASSON

AND

ROBERT N. ESSICK

VOLUME I

PLATES DESIGNED AND ENGRAVED BY BLAKE

PUBLISHED BY
THE AMERICAN BLAKE FOUNDATION
AT
ILLINOIS STATE UNIVERSITY
NORMAL, ILLINOIS
1972

Copyright © 1972 by The American Blake Foundation

All rights reserved. No part of this book may be reproduced or transmitted in any form or by any means, electronic or mechanical including photocopying, recording or by any information storage and retrieval system, without permission in writing from the Publisher.

First Published 1972 by The American Blake Foundation
The Department of English
Illinois State University
Normal, Illinois 61761

International Standard Book Number: O-913130-02-8 Limited Edition, Cloth
International Standard Book Number: O-913130-01-x Paper
Library of Congress Catalogue Card Number: 72-82993

Printed in the United States of America by Illinois Graphics

The prospectus for *The Royal Universal Family Bible* is quoted through the permission of the Curators of the Bodleian Library, Oxford University.

The plates from Thomas Commins' *An Elegy Set To Music* are reproduced by the permission of the Trustees of the British Museum.

The plates from Mary Wollstonecraft's *Original Stories*, William Hayley's *Little Tom the Sailor*, Robert John Thornton's The *Pastorals of Virgil, Remember Me!*, and plates 4 & 5 from Hayley's *Designs to a Series of Ballads*, are reproduced by the permission of the Princeton University Library.

Plates 7-8 from Hayley's *Designs to a Series of Ballads* and plates 1-3 from Hayley's 1805 *Ballads* are reproduced by the permission of the Henry E. Huntington Library, San Marino, California.

Plates from *The Prologue and Characters of Chaucer's Pilgrims* and the first proof sheet from Robert John Thornton's *The Pastorals of Virgil* are reproduced by the permission of the National Gallery of Art, Rosenwald Collection.

The plates from Edward Young's *Night Thoughts* are reproduced by the permission of Professor Robert N. Essick, Pasadena, California.

Plates from William Hayley's *Life of Cowper* and from *The Royal Universal Family Bible* are reproduced from the collection of The American Blake Foundation.

To
LESSING J. ROSENWALD

THE AMERICAN BLAKE FOUNDATION

A public non-profit educational trust established June 7, 1970 to support and encourage interest in William Blake, English poet and artist (1757-1827), by the creation of a public research facility, by hosting annual symposia, by publishing inexpensive, but quality facsimiles, and by awarding research grants.

DIRECTORS

Dale J. Briggs
> Attorney-at-law
> Tulsa, Oklahoma

Stuart Curran
> The University of Wisconsin
> Madison, Wisconsin

Kay Parkhurst Easson
> Illinois State University
> Normal, Illinois

Roger R. Easson
> Illinois State University
> Normal, Illinois

Robert N. Essick
> San Fernando Valley State College
> Northridge, California

Robert F. Gleckner
> The University of California
> Riverside, California

John E. Grant
> The University of Iowa
> Iowa City, Iowa

Jean Hagstrum
> Northwestern University
> Evanston, Illinois

Joseph Holland
> Los Angeles, California

Karl Kroeber
> Columbia University
> New York, New York

Edward J. Rose
> The University of Alberta
> Edmonton, Canada

Robert R. Wark
> The Huntington Art Gallery
> San Marino, California

Winston Weathers
> The University of Tulsa
> Tulsa, Oklahoma

Joseph Anthony Wittreich, Jr.
> The University of Wisconsin
> Madison, Wisconsin

PREFACE

The first volume in this series deals with books, pamphlets, and in one case a broadside, containing Blake's original graphic designs which he invented and engraved to illustrate a text not by Blake himself. These prints are worthy, in themselves, of considerable attention from the scholarly community, and take on a much greater interest as one's awareness of Blake's full achievement expands. Certainly any evaluation of Blake as a designer-engraver must take into account his Wollstonecraft designs, the *Night Thoughts* engravings with their imagery suggestive of the illuminated books, and other illustrations reproduced here, a few of them for the first time. The subsequent two volumes completing this series will present, in one chronological sequence, all those book illustrations either engraved or designed by Blake. We hope that these volumes will provide information about some of the basic source materials for future studies of Blake as a graphic artist.

The *raison d'être* for this publication is the complete reproduction of Blake's commercial book illustrations, but we have also provided notes on the prints and bibliographic descriptions of the books in which they appear. This information, however, is not intended to constitute a catalogue raisonné. Nor is the present volume meant to replace the works of Russell, Binyon, Keynes, and Bentley & Nurmi, although considerable information included in our notes is not included in these earlier bibliographies.

THE BOOKS

In *Principles of Bibliographical Description* (New York, 1949) Fredson Bowers identifies the three main objectives of Descriptive Bibliography as the attempt "1) to furnish a detailed, analytical record of the physical characteristics of a book which would simultaneously serve as a trustworthy source of identification and as a medium to bring an absent book before a reader's eyes; 2) to provide an analytical investigation and an ordered arrangement of these physical facts which would serve as the prerequisite for textual criticism of the books described; 3) to approach both literary and printing or publishing history through the investigation and recording of appropriate details in a related series of books" (p. vii). Our use of these principles in describing the following books is obviously not directed towards textual criticism. We are interested primarily in the first of these bibliographical objectives because our prime concern is to assist the student of Blake's art in his study of the prints which accompany these books. Moreover, we are interested in the printing and publishing history of the volumes only in as much as we are interested in Blake's role in that enterprise. It is unusual for a catalogue of prints to enter into so careful and complete a description of books which contain the prints, but we believe that the blend of the Descriptive Bibliography and the Print Catalogue, which this work embodies, will facilitate a new awareness of these designs and their physical contexts.

One unhappy reality of the designs presented here is that they are better known as graphic art than as illustrations within particular books. As a consequence of the one-sided attention they have received in the past, it is not unusual to find copies of these interesting prints uncatalogued as Blake-related items, or to find the books in which they appear in circulating stacks. We hope that one rather immediate result of this study will be to identify these books for the curator, the collector, and the student, and thereby to bring to these books a renewed evaluation and an increased concern for their preservation and study.

Since our use of the tools of Descriptive Bibliography is primarily for purposes of identification, we have not pursued Bowers' concept of "ideal copy." Rather, we have described exactly what we have seen, in multiple copies when that was possible. We present this description in the following blocks of information: 1) Facsimile title-page transcriptions (engraved title-pages are reproduced); 2) Collational formulae; 3) Pagination formulae; 4) Complete contents lists; 5) Notes on printing history, on variants, on special bibliographical problems, and on pertinent articles and bibliographies. All copies we have examined are listed at the conclusion of the entry.

A few aspects of our descriptive method may require some explanation. Following Fredson Bowers' suggestion (pp. 213-22), we have used in the collational formulae the Greek letter pi, π, to indicate the presence of unsigned but direction-numbered leaves in a prefixed gathering. Any leaf or group of leaves appearing at the beginning of a book which is unsigned, and to which a signature cannot legitimately be assigned, but which is numbered or capable of numbering by inference, is designated by π. In one case, the 1802 *Designs for a Series of Ballads*, this practice has been extended to engravings which, by reason of the project's special nature, must be considered part of the collation. In a similar convention the Greek letter chi, χ, has been used in collational formulae to designate unsigned but direction-numbered leaves or gatherings within a book, in the midst of regularly signed gatherings, or at the end of a book. Square brackets, [ ], are used to indicate signatures or page numbers which are missing and which have been inferred. In an attempt to illustrate the context in which the prints appear we have provided extensive descriptions of the contents of the books. It may seem to some that this information is excessive and a waste of time, but we believe that many who study the prints may have little access to the books themselves. Consequently, in an attempt to place these books in proper relationship to the prints, we offer these listings of contents.

We hope that our readers will gently call our attention to errors in these descriptions and to the existence of important copies in original boards which we have not examined.

THE PLATES

Like most eighteenth century engravers of the English school, Blake was in the habit of etching his plates in their first stages of development. Even though many such plates by Blake and his contemporaries have more etched lines than engraved lines, the usual practice, continued here, is to call them "engravings." Any determination of the number of engraved lines compared to the number etched should be based upon an examination of an impression from the plate; reproductions are a less sure guide to the method used to produce individual lines.

Our primary concern in this volume is with the published states of the engravings. Unless otherwise noted, reproductions are of the first published state. We have noted the existence, and when known, the location, of pre-publication states, preliminary sketches, and other closely related materials.

The "design size" listed for each plate gives the maximum height and width, in that order, of the engraved surface, including engraved border designs but not including inscriptions or imprints outside the limits of the design itself. The distance from the bottom of the letters of the imprint to the bottom margin of the design is also given, except for the *Night Thoughts* engravings where the distance is measured from the bottom of the letters of the imprint to the lower margin of the text panel. Although this measurement is not a standard part of the bibliographer's repertoire, we believe that it can be helpful in telling the difference between a pre-publication proof without imprint and a print trimmed at the bottom. All measurements are in centimeters to the nearest millimeter. Except where noted otherwise, reproductions are approximately the size of the originals.

All inscriptions and imprints are recorded since they are often difficult to make out in reproductions. The horizontal positioning of inscriptions is noted ("left" or "right") only for those not centered relative to the vertical axis of the plate.

For each book described here, reference is made by the entry number of the work in question to the following standard bibliographies and catalogues:

> Archibald G. B. Russell, *The Engravings of William Blake* (London: Grant Richards Ltd. and Boston: Houghton Mifflin, 1912, reprinted New York: Benjamin Blom, 1968).
>
> Geoffrey Keynes, *A Bibliography of William Blake* (New York: The Grolier Club, 1921, reprinted New York: Kraus Reprint Co., 1969).
>
> Laurence Binyon, *The Engraved Designs of William Blake* (London: Ernest Benn Ltd. and New York: Charles Scribner's Sons, 1926, reprinted New York: Da Capo Press, 1967).
>
> G. E. Bentley, Jr. and Martin K. Nurmi, *A Blake Bibliography* (Minneapolis, Minn.: University of Minnesota Press, 1964).

Throughout the text these works are referred to as "Russell," "Keynes," "Binyon," and "Bentley & Nurmi" respectively.

We have included in this volume only those book illustrations designed and engraved by Blake which have some claim on our attentions as works of original graphic art. Following this principle, we have excluded from this volume the plates listed below, even though they are signed by Blake as designer and engraver.

> *Wedgwood's Catalogue of Earthenware and Porcelain* (N.p., n.d.). Eighteen plates signed by Blake as designer and engraver.
>
> Abraham Rees, *The Cyclopædia* (London, 1820). One plate ("Sculpture, Plate III") signed by Blake as designer and engraver.
>
> *The Pastorals of Virgil*, Thornton's edition (London, 1821). Six copper-plate engravings of classical busts and coins signed by Blake as designer and engraver. Blake's seventeen wood engravings in this work have, of course, been included in this volume.

By the very nature of their subjects, these plates are essentially copies of another artist's work, be it Wedgwood's crockery or classical statuary, and are therefore not works of original graphic art. The twenty-five plates listed above will be included in volume III of this publication with other examples of Blake's reproductive prints.

We have been most conservative in our acceptance of attributions. Except for *Little Tom the Sailor* and the second plate of *The Prologue and Characters of Chaucer's Pilgrims* (see entries for details on attribution), this volume includes only those prints signed by Blake as designer and engraver or ascribed to him in the book in which his work appears. Therefore, we have excluded from this volume the prints listed below sometimes attributed to Blake as designer and engraver.

> Jacob Bryant, *A New System, or an Analysis of Ancient Mythology* (London, 1774-1776). The "Vignette of the Deluge" at the end of the third volume has been attributed to Blake (see Russell, p. 191 and Bentley & Nurmi, p. 103), but the plate is signed by Basire as engraver, and no preliminary drawing is known. Blake may have drawn and engraved this design, but no substantial evidence has come to light to clearly determine the extent of his labors.
>
> Richard Gough, *Sepulchral Monuments in Great Britain* (London, 1786). Eight plates all signed with some form of "*Basire del. et. sc.*" are attributed to Blake as designer by B. H. Malkin in *A Father's Memoirs of His Child* (London, 1806), pp. xx-xxi. Keynes (pp. 197-98) attributes a total of twelve plates to Blake and adds six more in his *Blake Studies* (second edition, Oxford, 1971), p. 17. Keynes and Bentley & Nurmi (p. 119) suggest that Blake also engraved at least some of these plates, but lacking more evidence on this matter we have omitted them from this volume.
>
> Society of Antiquaries, *Vetusta Monumenta* (London, 1789). Two preliminary water colored drawings and several plates have been attributed to Blake (see Russell, p. 192). However, the drawings and all plates are signed by Basire. This may simply indicate the master's shop in which the work was done rather than the actual artist, but lacking further information these plates are excluded from this volume.
>
> *The Seaman's Recorder* (London, 1824-1825, but some copies dated 1827). Five plates signed "Blake sc." and one plate, the frontispiece to volume II showing the Monument to Nelson by Flaxman in St. Paul's Cathedral, signed "Blake del et sc." This last plate, however, is by its very nature a copy of another artist's work and thus not an original graphic design.

All works attributed to Blake listed above will be reproduced in the subsequent two volumes. A full index covering all three volumes will appear at the end of the third volume.

ACKNOWLEDGMENTS

The American Blake Foundation especially appreciates the generous support of the Illinois State University Foundation in financing the production of this volume. Without this assistance the publication of *William Blake: Book Illustrator* would have been greatly hindered. And this assistance is only one indication of the continuing encouragement of creativity and excellence that is the essence of the Illinois State University Foundation's influence in the academic community.

Though the American Blake Foundation cannot thank individually all those who have constantly supported its efforts, it would be remiss in failing to acknowledge the great faith which the administration of Illinois State University has shown. In this regard, special thanks must go to Arlan C. Helgeson, Dean of the Graduate School and Acting Dean of the Faculties; Milton Greenberg, Dean of the College of Arts and Sciences; Charles W. Bolen, Dean of the College of Fine Arts; Henry H. Adams, Head of the Department of English; and Harold D. Wilkins and Ronald V. Mays of the Illinois State University Foundation. And, to the faculty and friends of the Foundation in the Department of English, particularly Professors Irene T. Brosnahan, Leger N. Brosnahan, George R. Canning, John M. Heissler, John S. Hill, Robert D. Sutherland, Rodger L. Tarr, Ray Lewis White, and William C. Woodson, warmest appreciation for daily supporting these efforts. To Mrs. Eileen M. Brand, Secretary of the College of Arts and Sciences, especial gratitude for her labor and trust.

The authors are greatly indebted to the following scholars, librarians, and collectors who have generously helped us in our researches: Fred Cain of the Alverthorpe Gallery, Jenkintown, Pennsylvania; Earl E. Coleman of the Princeton University Library; Robert Dougan of the Henry E. Huntington Library, San Marino, California; John Featlo of the Bodleian Library, Oxford University; Robert S. Fraser of the Princeton University Library; Mary Isabel Frye of the Huntington Library; Robert F. Gleckner of the University of California at Riverside; Susan F. Hadida of Faustus Bibliographics Ltd., London; Christina M. Hanson of the Beinecke Rare Book and Manuscript Library, Yale University; Joseph Holland, Los Angeles, California; Peter J. Knapp of the Trinity College Library, Hartford Connecticut; Sir Geoffrey Keynes, Suffolk, England; Raymond Lister, Cambridge, England; Paul Needham of the Pierpont Morgan Library, New York City; Howard M. Nixon of the British Museum, London; Lessing J. Rosenwald; James Thorpe, Director of the Henry E. Huntington Library and Art Gallery, San Marino; Robert R. Wark, Curator of the Henry E. Huntington Art Gallery; Edwin Wolf 2nd of the Library Company of Philadelphia.

We owe special debts to G. E. Bentley Jr. of the University of Toronto who permitted us to survey his Blake collection and helped us extensively throughout the preparation of this book, to John E. Grant of the University of Iowa who provided us with important assistance on Young's *Night Thoughts*, and to Richard Vogler of San Fernando Valley State College who provided us with essential information on Thomas Commins' *An Elegy Set to Music* in the British Museum.

We also wish to thank the Trustees of The British Museum, London; The Henry E. Huntington Library and Art Gallery, San Marino, California; The Bodleian Library, Oxford University, Oxford, England; The Princeton University Library, Princeton, New Jersey; and the Rosenwald Collection of the National Gallery of Art, Washington D.C. for allowing us to reproduce materials from their collections in this volume.

Without the aid and support of Professor Jenijoy LaBelle, California Institute of Technology, and without the considerable editorial prowess of Professor Kay Parkhurst

xi

Easson in designing and shaping our efforts, this volume could not have been successfully completed. Though Kay has often been the silent third member of this research team, her active assistance and participation have lent beauty to our researches.

                                              Roger R. Easson
                                              Robert N. Essick
                                                San Marino, California
                                                        1972

TABLE OF ABBREVIATIONS

References to the collections examined are made by the following abbreviations.

- ABF   The American Blake Foundation, The Department of English, Illinois State University, Normal, Illinois.
- BM   The British Museum, London.
- GEB   Collection of Prof. G. E. Bentley, Jr., Toronto.
- HEH   Henry E. Huntington Library and Art Gallery, San Marino, California.
- I   The University of Illinois Library, Urbana, Illinois.
- N   The Newberry Library, Chicago, Illinois.
- P   Princeton University Library, Princeton, New Jersey.
- R   Lessing J. Rosenwald Collection of the Library of Congress and the National Gallery of Art, Alverthorpe Gallery, Jenkintown, Pennsylvania.
- RNE   Collection of Prof. Robert N. Essick, Pasadena, California.
- UCLA   University of California Library, Los Angeles, California.
- UW   University of Washington Library, Seattle, Washington.
- W   Collection of Edwin Wolf 2nd, Jenkintown, Pennsylvania.

References to other collections are given by full name and city.

CONTENTS
VOLUME I

THE DESCRIPTIONS

I.	John Herries: THE ROYAL UNIVERSAL FAMILY BIBLE, 1780 & 1784.	1
II.	Thomas Commins: AN ELEGY SET TO MUSIC, 1786.	8
III.	Mary Wollstonecraft: ORIGINAL STORIES, 1791 & 1796.	9
IV.	Edward Young: NIGHT THOUGHTS, 1797.	13
V.	William Hayley: LITTLE TOM THE SAILOR, 1800.	29
VI.	William Hayley: DESIGNS TO A SERIES OF BALLADS, 1802.	31
VII.	William Hayley: THE LIFE AND POSTHUMOUS WRITINGS OF WILLIAM COWPER, 1803 & 1804.	36
VIII.	William Hayley: BALLADS, 1805.	41
IX.	THE PROLOGUE AND CHARACTERS OF CHAUCER'S PILGRIMS, 1812.	45
X.	Robert John Thornton: THE PASTORALS OF VIRGIL, 1821.	48
XI.	REMEMBER ME! 1825 & 1826.	53

THE PLATES

I.	John Herries: THE ROYAL UNIVERSAL FAMILY BIBLE	I. pl. 1
II.	Thomas Commins: AN ELEGY SET TO MUSIC	II. pl. 1
	Title-page	II. pl. 2
III.	Mary Wollstonecraft: ORIGINAL STORIES	III. pls. 1B, 2B, 3A-6A
IV.	Edward Young: NIGHT THOUGHTS	IV. pls. 1-43
V.	William Hayley: LITTLE TOM THE SAILOR	V. pls. 1-4
VI.	William Hayley: DESIGNS TO A SERIES OF BALLADS, 1802	VI. pls. 1-12
VII.	William Hayley: THE LIFE AND POSTHUMOUS WRITINGS OF WILLIAM COWPER	VII. pl. 1A
VIII.	William Hayley: BALLADS, 1805.	VIII. pls. 1A-3A, 4-5
IX.	THE PROLOGUE AND CHARACTERS OF CHAUCER'S PILGRIMS	IX. pls. 1-2
X.	Robert John Thornton: THE PASTORALS OF VIRGIL	X. proof sheet, nos. 1-17
XI.	REMEMBER ME!	XI. pl. 1
	Title-page	XI. pl. 2

I. John Herries:
THE ROYAL UNIVERSAL FAMILY BIBLE 1780 & 1784.

TITLE-PAGE, Volume I:

THE | ROYAL UNIVERSAL | FAMILY BIBLE; | OR, A COMPLETE LIBRARY OF | DIVINE KNOWLEDGE: | CONTAINING THE SACRED TEXT OF THE | Old and New Testaments, | WITH THE | APOCRYPHA AT LARGE; | ILLUSTRATED WITH | NOTES, CRITICAL, HISTORICAL, THEOLOGICAL AND PRACTICAL, | WHEREIN | The difficult Passages are explained, the seeming Contradictions reconciled, the Mis-translations corrected, | the deistical Objections refuted, and the Sacred Scriptures represented in their original Purity, | as the only Means of reconciling offending Man to his offended God. | WITH | PRACTICAL REFLECTIONS ON EACH CHAPTER. | The whole calculated to promote the Interest of Virtue and Piety, and make Men wise unto | Salvation. | TO WHICH IS ADDED |

I. At the End of each Book a Connection between Civil and Sacred History. | II. An Account of the great Men who flourished in the Hea- | then Nations in those Times, their Characters and Wri- | tings. | III. The State of Religion in the Heathen Nations, before | the Incarnation. | IV. Ancient and Modern Geography compared, shewing the | Difference in the Names of Places since the Christian Æra. | V. An Explanation of the Duty of all the Officers mentioned | in the Old and New Testaments.

VI. An Explanation of all the Scripture Terms, Names, and | Phrases. | VII. The History of the Old and New Testaments connected. | VIII. An Explanation of the Divine Offices used in the Jewish | Church, both before and after the Captivity. | IX. A Reconcilation of Sacred Chronology with the Records | of the Heathens. | X. A complete Concordance to the Old and New Testaments. | XI. A Critical and Historical Account of all the English Trans- | lations of the Bible. | XII. A complete Index to the Bible. |

[rule] | By the Reverend JOHN HERRIES, A.M. and Others. | [rule] | *Search the Scriptures.* John v. 39. | *All Scripture is given by the Inspiration of God, and is profitable for Doctrine, for Reproof, for Correction, and for* | *Instruction in Righteousness.* II. Tim. iii. 16. | [rule] | VOL. I. | [rule] | LONDON: | PRINTED FOR FIELDING AND WALKER, PATER-NOSTER-ROW, | MDCCLXXX.

    NOTE: The lines beginning with the words "FAMILY," "Old," "NOTES," "PRACTICAL," "TO," "By," "LONDON," and "MDCCLXXX." are printed in red.

        The 1780 title-page to Volume I which appears in the ABF and GEB copies is replaced in the BM, Harvard, and Toronto Public Library copies with a variant title-page. This variant has a new imprint reading "LONDON: | PRINTED FOR J. FIELDING No. 23, PATER-NOSTER-ROW, | MDCCLXXXI." This 1781 title-page is identical in all other respects. The general title-page to the second volume usually bears this 1781 imprint and differs only in a changed volume number. In all copies examined, the 1780 imprint never appeared at the beginning of the second volume. The Toronto Public Library copy has a later variant which again is identical except for the imprint which now reads: "PRINTED FOR JOHN FIELDING, Nº. 23, PATER-NOSTER ROW. | MDCCLXXXIV."

TITLE-PAGE, for the New Testament located in Volume II:
THE | NEW TESTAMENT | OF OUR | LORD AND SAVIOUR | JESUS CHRIST; | WITH | NOTES, | CRITICAL, HISTORICAL, AND THEOLOGICAL, | AND | PRACTICAL REFLECTIONS | ON | EACH CHAPTER. | THE WHOLE CALCULATED TO PROMOTE THE INTEREST OF VIRTUE AND PIETY, | AND MAKE MEN WISE UNTO SALVATION. | [rule] | BY THE REVEREND | JOHN HERRIES, A.M. | AND OTHERS. | [rule] | LONDON: | PRINTED FOR J. FIELDING, No. 23, PATER-NOSTER-ROW. | MDCCLXXXI.

>NOTE: The title-page in the BM and Toronto Public Library copies has been reset. It is the same except for the imprint which now reads "LONDON: | PRINTED FOR J. FIELDING, No. 23, PATER-NOSTER ROW. | M.DCC.LXXXV."

COLLATION: Vol. I: 2°: [a]² b² B-7T² 7U¹: 314 leaves + 59 plates. 24.5 × 38 cm.
Vol. II: 2°: [7U2] B-3Y² [3Z]² 4A-7C² χ²: 283 leaves + 41 plates.

PAGINATION: Lacking page numbers except for the single leaf of the Introduction in Volume I, [a2]. This leaf bears the odd pagination of "[i]" on the recto and " iv " on the verso. It would seem that the "[i]" may have originally been a brackted small roman numeral three, [iii], and somehow the external numerals have been lost.

>NOTE: In theory at least, it is possible to date the fascicles by an analysis of the dates within the imprints upon the engravings. The plates were not always published with the chapter and verse they illustrated, but were to be correctly arranged in the binding process. These dates indicate that the weekly publication took place with great regularity, but not without inconsistency. For example, 3 plates—maps—are without an imprint, and thus their fascicles cannot be properly placed. On the other hand, some plates carry identical dates: the dates August 4, 1781, December 22, 1781, and January 5, 1782 each appear on two plates. Only the December date seems designed to compensate for the absence of a fascicle published during the following week. For the first 98 weeks of this schedule the publication dates reflected in the imprints vary only 7 times in the omission of the following dates: January 4, 1781, July 21, 1781, October 20, 1781 October 27, 1781, December 29, 1781, and February 9, 1782. These missing weeks are partially compensated for by the 3 undated fascicles and the 3 duplicated dates above. At the end of the schedule the regularity ceases, for fascicle 99 was apparently published a month late on April 27, 1782, and the last fascicle 3 months later, July 27, 1782. Blake's plate is published as part of the ninety-third fascicle but bound within the ninety-fifth.
>
>The second volume begins within fascicle 53 and the New Testament begins with fascicle 76. Fifty plates are unsigned by either engraver or designer. Only 9 plates are signed by a designer: 5 carry the name Dodd, while 3 list D. Jenkins as both designer and engraver. Blake's plate is thus one of 4 that are both designed and engraved by the same hand.
>
>The ABF copy, complete with 100 plates, shows 56 plates numbered in an attempt to identify the publication sequence of the engravings. These numerals are often clumsily scratched into the copper plate and are completely unreliable when it comes to determining the relationship between the engravings and their original sequence of publication. The directions to the binder, found on the verso of 7C2, are not to be trusted either. Not only is the sequence found there not chronological, it is also not indicative of the final sequence the plates were to take in the finished book. Further, the directions to the binder list 101 engravings when there are only 100 engravings including the frontispiece. The error occurs when the same verse, Mark xvi,

12, is listed as having two illustrations: "53. Christ appearing to two of his Disciples" and "76. Christ sending two of his Disciples to prepare for the Passover." The design itself is sufficently ambiguous to fit either description.

While Blake himself was not intimately involved in the publication of this volume, the printing history is sufficiently involved to warrant close examination. The publication of *The Royal Universal Family Bible* is further complicated by a change in publishers in the midst of the weekly issuance of the fascicles. The project was apparently begun in 1781 by the firm of Fielding and Walker, and all the engravings printed between May 27, 1780 and March 3, 1781 carry the imprint *Fielding and Walker*. However, with the forty-second fascicle, dated March 10, 1781, the Walker is dropped. Consequently, the general title-page of the second volume, which is contained in fascicle 53, reflects this change as do all later variants of the imprint.

The Herries' Bible, as this work is occasionally labeled at the top of the engraved maps within, was apparently issued at least three times. The first issue was the weekly publication of the fascicles begun in May of 1781. This issue is marked by the presence of the 1780 Fielding and Walker title-page in Vol. I. Fielding reissued the volume in 1782 as the prospectus transcribed below from the John Johnson Collection indicates, offering it both in weekly parts and in two bound states complete. This second issue is marked by the absence of the 1780 title-page and the insertion of a new title-page with the 1781 variant imprint. A third and much later issue exists in only one known copy in the Toronto Public Library. Apparently Fielding reissued Herries' Bible in 1784 and 1785 for, while this copy carries the 1781 title-page in Vol. I, the general title-page to the second volume carries the 1784 variant described above, and the New Testament title-page carries the 1785 imprint. The collation of this issue is also somewhat different: Vol. I.: 2°: [a]² b¹ B-7T² 7U¹. Vol. II.: [7U²] B-3Y² [3X]² 3Z-6I² [6K]² 6L-6Q² 6P²(−6P2 = b1) 6R-7C². The b² quire, which in the ABF copy carries the note "VOL. I." in the signature, has been reduced to a single leaf containing only the "Tables of Scripture Measures." This single leaf seems to have been printed as 6P2, for this leaf is absent in the Toronto Public Library copy, and the verso of 6P1 bears offsetting which matches the recto of the new b1. In the GEB copy the b² quire appears in Vol. II after the 7C² quire.

The Royal Universal Family Bible is printed on a fine laid paper showing, centered on one half of the sheet, a simple fleur-de-lis and, centered on the other half, the initials IV. According to A. H. Shorter's *Paper Mills and Paper Makers in England, 1495-1800* (Hilversum, Holland, 1957), many papers with these initials were imported to England from the French paper mill of J. Villedary during the last half of the eighteenth century (p. 56). However, no exact identification of this watermark has been possible.

CONTENTS: Since there are no page numbers, signatures will be used in their place with the letter "*r*" indicating recto and the letter "*v*" indicating verso: [a1] *r title-page*. [a1] *v blank*. [a2] *r&v* Introduction. b1 *r&v* Tables of Scripture Measures, Weights, and Coins: with an appendix, Containing the Method of calculating its Measure of Surface, hitherto wanting in Treatises on this Subject. By the Right Reverend Richard Lord Bishop of Peterborough. b2 *r* A Table of Time. | A Table of Officers and Conditions of Men. b2 *v* The Names and Order of all the Books of the Old and New Testament, with the Number of their Chapters, Verses, &c. B1 *r* The First Book of Moses Called Genesis. Dd1 *r* The Second Book of Moses, Called Exodus. Rr2 *v* The Third Book of Moses, Called Leviticus. Ddd1 *r* The Fourth Book of Moses, Called Numbers. Qqq1 *r* The Fifth Book of Moses, Called Deuteronomy. 4C2 *r* The Book of Joshua. 4K2 *r* The Book of

Judges. 4R1 *v* The Book of Ruth. 4S1 *v* The First Book of Samuel, Otherwise Called The First Book of the Kings. 5C1 *v* The Second Book of Samuel, Otherwise Called The Second Book of the Kings. 5I2 *v* The First Book of the Kings, Commonly Called The Third Book of the Kings. 5Q1 *r* The Second Book of the Kings, Commonly Called The Fourth Book of the Kings. 5X2 *v* The First Book of the Chronicles. 6D1 *v* The Second Book of the Chronicles. 6K2 *r* Ezra. 6M2 *v* The Book of Nehemiah. 6P2 *r* The Book of Esther. 6R1 *v* The Book of Job. 6Z1 *r* The Book of Psalms. 7N2 *r* A Dissertation on the Ancient Hebrew Poetry and Music. 7N2 *v* The Proverbs. 7R2 *v* Ecclesiastes; or, the Preacher. 7T1 *v* The Song of Solomon . 7U1 *r* A Dissertation on the Wisdom of Solomon. 7U2 *r* title-page to the second volume. 7U2 *v blank*. B1 *r* The Book of the Prophet Isaiah. L1 *v* The Book of the Prophet Jeremiah. X2 *v* The Lamentations of Jeremiah. Y2 *v* A Dissertation on the Style and Manner of the Prophets; Chiefly compiled and translated from Dr. Lowth, the present Bishop of London's *Prælectiones Academicæ de Sacra Poesi Hebræorum* [Part I]. Z1 *r* The Book of the Prophet Ezekiel. Ii2 *v* A Dissertation on the Style and Manner . . . [Part II]. Kk1 *r* The Book of Daniel. Nn1 *r* Hosea. Oo2 *r* A Dissertation on the Style and Manner . . . [Part III]. Oo2 *v* Joel. Pp1 *v* A Dissertation on the Style and Manner . . . [Part IV]. Pp2 *r* Amos. Qq2 *v* A Dissertation on the Style and Manner . . . [Part V]. Rr1 *r* Obadiah. Rr1 *v* A Dissertation on the Style and Manner . . . [Part VI]. Rr1 *v* Jonah. Rr2 *v* Micah. Ss2 *v* A Dissertation on the Style and Manner . . . [Part VII]. Ss2 *v* Nahum. Tt1 *v* A Dissertation on the Style and Manner . . . [Part VIII]. Tt1 *v* Habakkuk. Tt2 *v* A Dissertation on the Style and Manner . . . [Part IX]. Uu1 *r* Zephaniah. Uu2 *r* A Dissertation on the Style and Manner . . . [Part X]. Uu2 *r* Haggai. Xx1 *r* A Dissertation on the Style and Manner . . . [Part XI]. Xx1 *r* Zechariah. Yy2 *v* A Dissertation on the Style and Manner . . . [Part XII]. Yy2 *v* Malachi. Zz1 *v* A Dissertation on the Style and Manner . . . [Part XIII]. Zz2 *v* The Apocrypha At Large; Illustrated with Notes, Critical, Historical, Moral, and Theological. I. Esdras. Bbb2 *r* II. Esdras. Eee2 *r* Tobit. Fff2 *v* Judith. Hhh1 *v* The Rest of the Chapters of the Book of Esther, which are found neither in the Hebrew, nor in the Chaldee. Hhh2 *v* The Wisdom of Solomon. Kkk2 *r* The Wisdom of Jesus the Son of Sirach, or Ecclesiasticus. Ppp1 *r* Baruch. Ppp2 *v* The Song of the Three Holy Children. Qqq1 *r* The History of Susanna. Qqq1 *v* The History of the Destruction of Bel and the Dragon. Qqq2 *r* The Prayer of Manasses, King of Judah, when he was holden captive in Babylon. Qqq2 *v* The First Book of the Maccabees. Uuu1 *r* The Second Book of the Maccabees. Yyy2 *r* Connection of the History of the Old and New Testament. [Zzz] 1 *r* title-page to the New Testament. [Zzz]1 *v blank* [Zzz]2 *r* The Gospel According to St. Matthew. 4G1 *r* Connection of the History of the Old and New Testament [Part II]. 4G1 *v* The Gospel According to St. Mark. 4L1 *v* Connection of the History of the Old and New Testament [Part III]. 4L2 *r* The Gospel According to St. Luke. 4T1 *r* Connection of the History of the Old and New Testament [Part IV]. 4T1 *v* The Gospel According to St. John. 5B1 *r* The Acts of the Apostles. 4I1 *v* The Epistle of Paul the Apostle to the Romans. 5M1 *v* The First Epistle of Paul the Apostle to the Corinthians. 5P1 *r* A Short History of the Propagation of the Gospel. [*Continued from the Additional Notes on the Acts of the Apostles.*] 5P1 v The Second Epistle of Paul the Apostle to the Corinthians. 5R1 *v* A Short History . . . [Part II].

5R2 *r* The Epistle of Paul the Apostle to the Galatians. 5S2 *r* A Short History... [Part III]. 5S2 *v* The Epistle of Paul the Apostle to the Ephesians. 5T2 *v* A Short History... [Part IV]. 5U1 *r* The Epistle of Paul the Apostle to the Philippians. 5U2 *v* A Short History... [Part V]. 5X1 *r* The Epistle of Paul the Apostle to the Colossians. 5X2 *v* A Short History... [Part VI]. 5X2 *v* The First Epistle of Paul the Apostle to the Thessalonians. 5Y2 *r* A Short History... [Part VII]. 5Y2 *v* The Second Epistle of Paul the Apostle to the Thessalonians. 5Z1 *r* A Short History... [Part VIII]. 5Z1 *v* The First Epistle of Paul the Apostle to Timothy. 6A1 *r* A Short History... [Part IX]. 6A1 *v* The Second Epistle of Paul the Apostle to Timothy. 6B1 *r* A Short History... [Part X]. 6B1 *v* The Epistle of Paul the Apostle to Titus. 6B2 *v* Profane History During the Period of the Travels and Preaching of the Gospel By the Apostles [Part I]. 6B2 *v* The Epistle of Paul the Apostle to Philemon. 6C1 *r* Profane History... [Part II]. 6C1 *v* The Epistle of Paul the Apostle to the Hebrews. 6E2 *r* Profane History... [Part III]. 6E2 *v* The General Epistle of James. 6F2 *r* Profane History... [Part IV]. 6F2 *v* The First Epistle General of Peter. 6G2 *r* Profane History... [Part V]. 6G2 *v* The Second Epistle General of Peter. 6H1 *v* Profane History... [Part VI]. 6H2 *r* The First Epistle General of John. 6I1 *v* Profane History... [Part VII]. 6I2 *r* The Second Epistle of John. 6I2 *v* Profane History... [Part VIII]. 6K1 *r* The Third Epistle General of John. 6K1 *r* Profane History... [Part IX]. 6K1 *v* The General Epistle of Jude. 6K2 *v* Profane History... [Part X]. 6L1 *r* The Revelation of St. John The Divine. 6Q1 *r* Ancient and Modern Geography Compared; Shewing the Difference in the Names of Places since the Christian Æra. 6S1 *v* Geographical Index. 6S2 *r* A Brief Concordance or Index to the Whole Bible. Shewing the more easily to find out the most useful Passages. 7B1 *r* A Critical and Historical Account of English Translations of the Bible. 7C1 *v* A Critical Index. 7C2 *r* [an advertisement] This Day is Published the whole works of Flavius Josephus. 7C2 *v* Directions for the Binder. 7C2 *v* [an advertisement] Bartholomew Adams. Book-binder. χ1 A List of Subscribers to Herries's Royal Universal Family Bible.

> NOTE: A prospectus for the *Royal Universal Family Bible* (in the John Johnson Collection of Literary Ephemera at the Bodleian Library, Oxford), apparently published in the May issue of the *Universal Magazine*, 1782, reads in part as follows:

ROYAL FAMILY BIBLE, ON A PLAN ENTIRELY NEW, AND NEVER BEFORE ATTEMPTED IN ANY LANGUAGE; *Being printed on a* large new Letter, *superfine Paper, and illustrated with* ONE HUNDRED *of the most elegant* COPPER-PLATES *that were ever yet given in the* Sacred Scriptures; *and those* CHRISTIAN FAMILIES *who are desirous of becoming possessed of this valuable Work, are requested to peruse the following Proposal.*

On Saturday, the 1st of June, 1782, will be published, Price Six-Pence, Embellished with a most elegant FRONTISPIECE, designed by DODD and engraved by WALKER. Number I. (To be continued Weekly) OF THE ROYAL UNIVERSAL FAMILY BIBLE; OR A COMPLETE LIBRARY OF DIVINE KNOWLEDGE....

The whole of this Work, being just printed off, may be had complete in One Hundred Numbers, at 6d each; or elegantly bound in one Volume Calf, lettered, 2l. 18s. and 3l. 3s. bound in two Volumes.

*** Any Person may be supplied with one or more Numbers at a Time till the whole is completed.

By the Reverend JOHN HERRIES, A.M. and Others.

LONDON:

Printed for JOHN FIELDING, No. 23, *Pater-noster-Row*, and sold by all the Booksellers and News-Carriers in Town and Country.

CONDITIONS. I. THAT this work shall be beautifully printed in Folio, on fine paper, and an excellect new letter cast on purpose for this work. II. That the whole will be completed in *One Hundred Numbers*, making Two elegant Volumes in folio, or the overplus given *gratis*. III. That each number shall contain three sheets of letter press, and an elegant copper-plate print of some striking part of the Scripture History, from original drawings by

Dodd, or from the most capital foreign paintings and prints. IV. The historical plates shall be engraved by *Walker, Collyer, Thornthwaite, Cooke, Heath, Grignion, Jenkins, Burrell, Page,* and other the most ingenious artists, and the maps by *Palmer, Ellis, Bowen,* and *Lodge,* and the whole ornamented with curious borders by Mr. *Clowes.* V. That every historical plate will be dedicated by the author to one of the bishops, or the other dignified clergy, with their coats of arms elegantly engraved at the bottom of each print. VI. That every reader may form a judgment of the execution of the work, the first number may be returned if not approved of. VII. A list of the subscribers shall be printed and delivered *gratis* in the last number. VIII. In the first number the publisher will give a note of hand, engaging to deliver the overplus *gratis,* if the work should exceed the hundred numbers proposed. . . .

A LIST OF THE ELEGANT COPPER-PLATES IN HERRIES's ROYAL FAMILY BIBLE.

[The following list of plates is identical to that found in the Directions for the Binder, but the numbers are here added by the eds.]

The Engraving of which has cost the Publisher upwards of Seven Hundred Pounds, and are not to be equalled for Nobleness of Design, and Correctness of Engraving, in any other Bible yet extant.

FRONTISPIECE.—STUDY with a Book in one Hand and a Pen in the other; on her right Hand, CANDOUR looking with a placid Eye; on the left, WISDOM directing STUDY. On the left of WISDOM is CHARITY and BENEVOLENCE, two infant Figures, embracing each other. Above is TRUTH crowned with Rays of Glory, pointing to a pleasant Grove before the Gates of a Temple, thereby insinuating that Pleasure attends us in our Journey to Heaven. Behind, on the right, is FALSHOOD, ENVY, IGNORANCE, and FOLLY falling headlong into the bottomless Pit. [1] Adam placed by the Lord in the Garden of Eden. [2] Cain killing his Brother Abel. [3] The Angel appearing unto Hagar. [4] Abraham meeting Rebekah. [5] Abimelech making a Covenant with Isaac. [6] The Vision of Jacob's Ladder. [7] Joseph sold into Egypt by the Midianites. [8] Pharoah drowned in the Red Sea. [9] The Lord appears upon Mount Sinai to Moses. [10] The consecrating Aaron. [11] Moses coming down from Mount Sinai, with the two Tables. [12] The Free Gifts for the Tabernacle. [13] Nadab and Abihu burnt. [14] The Children of Israel stopping at the Brook of Eshcol. [15] Moses maketh a Serpent of Brass. [16] Joshua at the Brink of Jordan with the Ark. [17] Acan stoned in the Valley of Achor. [18] Joshua commanding the Sun to stand still. [19] Sisera killed in a Tent by Jael. [20] The Angel appeareth unto Gideon. [21] Gideon's army drinking at the Well of Harod. [22] Sampson killing the Lion. [23] Sampson carrying away the Gates of Gaza. [24] Boaz taketh notice of Ruth gleaning in his Fields. [25] David killing Goliah. [26] David findeth Saul asleep in his Tent. [27] David seeing Bathsheba bathing. [28] Joab killing Absalom. [29] The Fire of the Lord consuming the Sacrifice of Elijah. [30] Elijah bid to go down to Moab by the Angel. [31] Jehoram slain by Jehu in his Chariot. [32] Manasseh worshipping a graven Image of the Grove. [33] David beholdeth the Angel of the Lord. [34] God's Acceptance of Solomon's Prayer. [35] Ahab slain by an Arrow. [36] The Angel destroying the Assyrians in their Camp. [37] The building of the House of the Lord forwarded by Joshua, &c. [38] Mordecai arrayed by Haman in the King's Apparel. [39] Job's Wife desiring him to curse God and die. [40] Solomon's Temple. [41] Jeremiah drawn out of the Dungeon. [42] The Vision of the Cherubim. [43] Nebuchadnezzar eating the Grass of the Field. [44] The Vision of the four Beasts to Daniel. [45] Tobit drawing the Fish out of the Water. [46] Tobit curing his Father of Blindness. [47] David anointed by Samuel. [48] The Vision of the dried Bones. [49] Jonah entering the City of Nineveh. [50] Daniel destroys the Bell and the Dragon. [51] The Nations around Mount Sion fall upon the Jews. [52] St. Matthew. [53] Christ appearing to two of his Disciples. [54] Herod's Cruelty at Bethlem, [55] Christ carrying his Cross. [56] Christ and the Woman of Samaria. [57] Job reproved by Elihu. [58] The Feast of the Loaves and Fishes. [59] The Viper on St. Paul's Hand. [60] Christ's Ascension. [61] The Judgment of Solomon. [62] The stoning of Zechariah. [63] Shadrach, Meshech and Abednego in the fiery Furnace. [64] God's Covenant signified by the Rainbow. [65] Judith giving the Head of Holofernes to her Maid. [66] The Resurrection of Christ. [67] Map of Egypt. (68) Map of the Holy Land. [69] Peter released from Prison by an Angel. [70] Isaiah prophesying unto Hezekiah. [71] Elijah fed by Ravens at the Brook of Cherith. [72] A Map shewing the Parts of the Globe settled by the Sons of Noah. [73] The prodigal Son feeding Swine. [74] Christ sending forth the Apostles to preach the Gospel. [75] God appearing to Moses in the burning Bush. [76] Christ sending two of his Disciples to prepare the Passover. [77] The stoning of Stephen. [78] St. John. [79] St. Mark. [80] The Parable of the Sower. [81] Christ talking with Moses and Elias. [82] Christ tempted by Satan in the Wilderness. [83] Christ raising the Dead. [84] Christ betrayed by Judas. [85] Christ baptized by John in the River Jordan. [86] St. Luke. [87] The crucifying of Christ and the two Thieves. [88] Eleazar obliged to eat Swines Flesh. [89] Plan of the Temple of Jerusalem. [90] Jesus bidding Zaccheus to come from the Sycamore Tree. [91] The Vision of the seven golden Candlesticks. [92] A Map of the World as divided between Noah's Sons, according to the Ancients. [93] Christ healing the Leper. [94] The Sabbath-breaker stoned. [95] The seven Angels with the seven Vials of the Wrath of God. [96] The fourth Angel giving John the Book to eat. [97] The death of Antiochus. [98] A Map of the Expedition of Shalmaneser against the Israelites. [99] View of Jerusalem. [100] The Vision of the New City.

PLATES

One hundred intaglio copper-plate engravings. Of the five plates engraved by Blake, one is also designed by him.

1. Vol. II, facing the second page of Revelations, listed in the directions to the binder as "[plate] 91. The vision of the seven golden Candlesticks."
    INSCRIPTION above the design within the decorative border: REVELATIONS, | Chap. 1 Ver, 12 & 13
    INSCRIPTION below design, right, within the border: *Blake. d & sc*
    INSCRIPTION below the design on either side of the heraldic shield:

To the Reverend	*Richd Dobbs, A.M.*
Dean of	Connor,
This PLATE is most	*humbly Inscribed,*
By his most Obedient	*Servant Jno Herries*

    IMPRINT below the heraldic shield: *Published Feby 23 1782 by J Fielding Paternoster Row*
    DESIGN SIZE: 16.1 × 10.5 cm. (inner design signed by Blake); 25.7 × 16.9 cm. (including decorative border). The imprint is .2 cm. below the heraldic shield.
    NOTE: The decorative border appears to have been engraved on the same plate as Blake's inner design. The prospectus in the John Johnson Collection of Literary Ephemera in the Bodleian Library, quoted in part above, states that "the whole [will be] ornamented with curious borders by Mr. *Clowes*." It seems likely that each engraver was given a border design (by Clowes) and a central design, in which case Blake would have engraved the border as well as his own design. The inscription "Palmer *scripsit*" beneath a small curved rule appears on the lower right corner of the frontispiece to the *Bible,* and it is possible that this third hand engraved the letters on Blake's plate as well. Blake's India ink drawing for the central design is in the BM Department of Prints and Drawings.
    We wish to thank Prof. G. E. Bentley, Jr. for pointing out the existence of the prospectus in the John Johnson Collection.

COPIES EXAMINED: ABF (first issue); BM (second issue: examined for us by Richard Vogler); GEB (first issue, with a contemporary signature dated "1783"); Toronto Public Library, Toronto, Ontario (third issue).
COPY REPRODUCED: ABF.
Russell, Keynes, and Binyon: not listed; Bentley & Nurmi #338.

II. Thomas Commins: AN ELEGY SET TO MUSIC, 1786.

TITLE-PAGE: Because this is a pamphlet of sheet music, there is no title-page as such. The first page of music, bearing the engraved title, is reproduced as plate II, 2.

COLLATION: No signatures. The pamphlet is composed of a cover-leaf bearing Blake's engraving, a disjunct leaf and two conjugate leaves, in that order. The cover-leaf is folded along the left edge creating a flap into which the other leaves are inserted: 4 leaves with 6 plates. 34 × 24 cm.

PAGINATION: 2pp. [1] 2-5 [6].

CONTENTS: 2pp. cover-leaf, verso *blank*. [1] An Elegy Set to Music. [6] *blank*.

PLATES

One intaglio copper-plate engraving, designed and engraved by Blake.

1. Vignette on the cover sheet.
   INSCRIPTION around lower part of the oval design: *W. Blake delt. & sculpt.*
   INSCRIPTION below design:
   > *The shatter'd bark from adverse winds*
   > *Rest in this peaceful haven finds*
   > *And when the storms of life are past*
   > *Hope drops her anchor here at last*

   IMPRINT beneath inscription: *Publish'd July 1, 1786 by J. Fentum No. 78 Corner of Salisbury Street, Strand*
   DESIGN SIZE: 17.3 × 13.8 cm. The imprint is 5.8 cm. below the design.
   NOTE: Keynes (p. 198) states that a sketch for the design "was in 1913 in the hands of Messrs. Robson." The present location of this sketch has not been traced.

COPY EXAMINED: BM Department of Prints and Drawings (examined for us by Richard Vogler).

COPY REPRODUCED: BM Department of Prints and Drawings.

Russell #4; Keynes #68; Binyon #10; Bentley & Nurmi #360.

III. Mary Wollstonecraft: ORIGINAL STORIES, 1791 & 1796.

TITLE-PAGE, the first edition with Blake's plates, 1791:
ORIGINAL STORIES | FROM | *REAL LIFE*; | WITH | CONVERSATIONS, | CALCULATED TO | REGULATE THE AFFECTIONS, | AND | FORM THE MIND | TO | TRUTH AND GOODNESS. | BY MARY WOLLSTONECRAFT. | [rule] | *LONDON:* | PRINTED FOR J. JOHNSON, NO. 72, ST. | PAUL'S CHURCH-YARD. | [rule] | 1791.

COLLATION: 12° : A^6 $B-H^{12}$ I^6 : 96 leaves + 6 plates. 16.8 × 10 cm.

PAGINATION: [i-iii] iv-vi [vii] viii [ix-xii] [1] 2-177 [178-180].

CONTENTS: p. [i] title-page. p. [ii] *blank*. p. [iii] Preface. p. [vii] Introduction. p. [ix] Contents. p. [1] text. p. [178] A catalogue of books composed for children and young persons, and generally used in the principal schools and academies in England.

TITLE-PAGE, the second edition with Blake's plates, 1796:
ORIGINAL STORIES | FROM | *REAL LIFE*; | WITH | CONVERSATIONS, | CALCULATED TO | REGULATE THE AFFECTIONS, | AND | FORM THE MIND TO | TRUTH AND | GOODNESS. | BY | MARY WOLLSTONECRAFT. | [rule] | A NEW EDITION. | [rule] | *LONDON:* | PRINTED FOR J. JOHNSON, NO. 72, St. Paul's | CHURCH-YARD. | [rule] | 1796.
> NOTE: In the Huntington copy the dash between "CHURCH" and "YARD" is only visible as the imprint of the un-inked type. Consequently, a variant state of the title-page may exist due to faulty inking or a broken type.

COLLATION: 12° : A^6 $B-G^{12}$ H^6 : 88 leaves + 6 plates. 16.8 × 10 cm.
> NOTE: The first gathering has an initial signature of A^2. A^1 is unsigned since it is the title-page.

PAGINATION: [i-iii] iv-vi [vii] viii [ix-xii] [1] 2-155 [156].

CONTENTS: p. [i] title-page. p. [ii] *blank*. p. [iii] Preface. p. [vii] Introduction. p. [ix] Contents. p. [1] text. p. [156] Books written by the same Author.
> NOTE: The text of *Original Stories* is composed of 25 chapters which make up this novel. In the traditional manner of the early novel, each chapter is headed by a summational title. As the volume has been reprinted in fairly recent years, these insignificant titles have not been transcribed here. Engraved on the upper right corner of each plate is a small word or number designed to instruct the binder where to place the plate within the 1791 edition. These instructions read respectively: *Frontispiece, P. 24, P. 74, P. 94, P. 111, P. 173*. Usually such instructions indicate the plate is to face the page designated; however, some copies have the plates inserted with their blank versos facing the page instead.
>
> The 1796 edition does not change these instructions even though the text is compressed from the original 177 pages in the 1791 edition to 155 pages in the 1796 edition. Consequently, in the 1796 edition, it is impossible for the last plate to be properly positioned since there is no page 173. This plate thus appears irregularly among the last eleven pages. In the Huntington Library copy, for example, it appears facing page 148. A further result of this compression is the failure of the last four plates to appear within the stories they illustrate.

PLATES

Six intaglio copper-plate engravings, all designed and engraved by Blake. Russell (p. 57) reports the existence of an early state of the pls. "prior to the first edition," herein described as the first state of pls. 1 and 2 only since they were in fact published with some copies of the book. Binyon lists this early state for the first pl. only. The reproductions in *Mary Wollstonecraft's Original Stories*, with an intro. by E. V. Lucas (London, 1906) are of the second state of pl. 1 and of the first states of pls. 3-6 (pl. 2 is not reproduced). We reproduce here the second states of pls. 1 and 2 and the first states of pls. 3-6. The preliminary wash drawings for all but pl. 5 are now in the Rosenwald Collection and are reproduced in William Godwin, *Memoirs of Mary Wollstonecraft*, ed. W. Clark Durant (London & New York, 1927). Also reproduced in this edition of the *Memoirs* are 5 designs never engraved, now in the Rosenwald Collection.

1A. Frontispiece facing the title-page, first published state appearing in the Rosenwald and UCLA copies of the 1791 ed. and in the HEH copy of the 1796 ed.
   INSCRIPTION above design, right: *Frontispiece.*
   INSCRIPTION below design, right: *Blake. d. & sc:*
   INSCRIPTION below design: *Look what a fine morning it is.—Insects, | Birds, & Animals, are all enjoying existence.*
   IMPRINT below inscription: *Published by J. Johnson, Septr 1st 1791.*
   DESIGN SIZE: 11.7 × 6.5 cm. The imprint is 1.8 cm. below the design.
   NOTE: This first published state is reproduced in Russell, pl. 4 and Raymond Lister, *William Blake: An Introduction to the Man and to His Work* (London, 1968), pl. 1.

1B. Frontispiece facing the title-page, second published state appearing in the HEH, I, N, RNE, and UW copies of the 1791 ed.
   INSCRIPTIONS, IMPRINT, AND DESIGN SIZE: as in first state.
   NOTE: The background in the second state has been darkened with the addition of dots and fine diagonal lines within the doorway. Heavy lines have been added around the door and crosshatching has been added to deepen the shadow on the lower portion of the women's dress.

1C. Frontispiece facing the title-page, third published state appearing in all copies examined of the 1796 ed. except for the HEH copy with the first state.
   ADDITIONAL INSCRIPTION below design, right, replacing the signature recorded above for the first state: *Blake. inv. & sc.*
   OTHER INSCRIPTIONS, IMPRINT, AND DESIGN SIZE: as in first state.
   NOTE: Almost the entire pl. in the third state has been darkened with crosshatching and deeper lines. The woman's dress has been lengthened so that it now covers all but the toe of her left foot, and the folds of the right girl's skirt have been reworked. Lines have been added to the woman's dress, particularly the bodice and arms. This third published state is reproduced in Geoffrey Keynes, ed., *William Blake's Engravings* (London, 1950), pl. 6.

2A. Facing p. 24, first published state appearing in the Rosenwald and UCLA copies of the 1791 ed. and in the HEH copy of the 1796 ed.
   INSCRIPTION above design, right: *P. 24.*
   INSCRIPTION below design: *The Dog strove to attract his attention.— | He said, Thou wilt not leave me!*

IMPRINT below inscription: *Published by J. Johnson, Sept. 1, 1791.*
DESIGN SIZE: 11.5 × 6.6 cm. The imprint is 2.2 cm. below the design.
> NOTE: This first published state is reproduced in Harrison R. Steeves, *Before Jane Austen: The Shaping of the English Novel in the Eighteenth Century* (London, 1966), p. 311. Sketches of similar designs appear in the lower left corner of p. 15 and center of p. 39 in Blake's *Notebook (Rossetti Manuscript).*

2B. Facing p. 24, second published state appearing in the HEH, I, N, P, RNE, and UW copies of the 1791 ed.
INSCRIPTIONS, IMPRINT, AND DESIGN SIZE: as in first state.
> NOTE: The floor, window, and upper left corner of the cell have been darkened in the second state with dots and crosshatching. A few lines have been added to the legs of the bed and the dog's left rear leg.

2C. Facing p. 24, third published state appearing in all copies examined of the 1796 ed. except for the HEH copy with the first state.
ADDITIONAL INSCRIPTION below design, right: *Blake.· inv. & sculp.*
OTHER INSCRIPTIONS, IMPRINT, AND DESIGN SIZE: as in first state.
> NOTE: The floor in the third state has been darkened. The first child's clothes have been darkened with heavy lines. The dog has been darkened with deeper lines. The Man's pants, hair, and the shadow, now extending onto his left shoulder, have been considerably darkened. This third published state is reproduced in A. Edward Newton, *A Magnificent Farce and Other Diversions of a Book-Collector* (London & Boston, 1921), facing p. 208 (with the preliminary drawing).

3A. Facing p. 74, first published state appearing in the 1791 ed.
INSCRIPTION above design, right: *P. 74.*
INSCRIPTION below design: *Indeed we are very happy!* ———
IMPRINT below inscription: *Published by J. Johnson, Sept. 1, 1791.*
DESIGN SIZE: 11.3 × 6.8 cm. The imprint is 2.1 cm. below the design.

3B. Facing p. 74, second published state appearing in the 1796 ed.
ADDITIONAL INSCRIPTION below design, right: *Blake. i &. s*
OTHER INSCRIPTIONS, IMPRINT, AND DESIGN SIZE: as in first state.
> NOTE: The floor and entire background in the second state have been darkened with dots and additional lines. The hair on all six figures has been considerably darkened with additional lines. The dresses of the two children on the left and the clothing of the man and boy have been darkened with additional lines and dots. More lines have been added to both chairs.

4A. Facing p. 94, first published state appearing in the 1791 ed. and the GEB copy of the 1796 ed., facing p. 82.
INSCRIPTION above design, right: *P. 94.*
INSCRIPTION below design: *Be calm, my child, remember that you | must do all the good you can the present day.*
IMPRINT below inscription: *Published by J. Johnson, Sept. 1, 1791.*
DESIGN SIZE: 11.8 × 6.6 cm. The imprint is 1.9 cm. below the design.

4B. Facing p. 94, second published state appearing in all copies examined of the 1796 ed. except for the GEB copy with the first state.
ADDITIONAL INSCRIPTION below design, right: *Blake in & sc*
OTHER INSCRIPTIONS, IMPRINT, AND DESIGN SIZE: as in first state.

NOTE: The trunk and foliage of the tree on the left in the second state have been darkened with lines and dots. Additional lines have been added to the woman's hat, hair, and dress. The hair of the girl on the left has been darkened. A few dots have been added just below the window on the building in the background.

5A. Facing p. 114, first published state appearing in the 1791 ed. and in the GEB copy of the 1796 ed., facing p. 100.
INSCRIPTION above design, right: *P. 114.*
INSCRIPTION below design: *Trying to trace the sound, I discovered | a little hut, rudely built.*
IMPRINT below inscription: *Published by J. Johnson, Sept.r 1, 1791.*
DESIGN SIZE: 12 × 6.4 cm. The imprint is 1.9 cm. below the design.

5B. Facing p. 114, second published state appearing in all copies examined of the 1796 ed. except for the GEB copy with the first state.
ADDITIONAL INSCRIPTION below design, right: *Blake. i. & sc.*
OTHER INSCRIPTIONS, IMPRINT, AND DESIGN SIZE: as in first state.
NOTE: The ruined arch in the right background, the woman's hat, the interior of the hut, the ruined column above the hut, the harper's arms, and the woman's left hand have all been darkened with additional dots in the second state. The woman's eyes have been partly closed. Lines have been added to the harper's knees, his left lapel, and to the left side of the chair. This second published state is reproduced in Binyon, pl. 5 (although the caption states that this is from the 1791 ed.), and in Geoffrey Keynes, ed., *William Blake's Engravings* (London, 1950), pl. 5.

6A. Facing p. 173, first published state appearing in the 1791 ed.
INSCRIPTION above design, right: *P. 173.*
INSCRIPTION below design: *Œconomy & Self-denial are necessary, in | every station, to enable us to be generous.*
IMPRINT below inscription: *Published by J. Johnson, Sept.r 1, 1791.*
DESIGN SIZE: 11.6 × 6.5 cm. The imprint is 2.2 cm. below the design.

6B. Irregularly placed in Chap. XXIV, second published state appearing in the 1796 ed.
ADDITIONAL INSCRIPTION below design, right: *Blake inv. sc.*
OTHER INSCRIPTIONS, IMPRINT, AND DESIGN SIZE: as in first state.
NOTE: Almost the entire engraving has been darkened with additional lines and dots in the second state, including particularly the background, the floor, the hats and dresses of the two women, the clothing and hair of the three seated figures, and the chair.

COPIES EXAMINED: GEB (1796 ed. with first state of pls. 4 and 5); HEH (1791 ed. with second state of pls. 1 and 2, 1796 ed. with first state of pls. 1 and 2); I (1791 ed. with second state of pls. 1 and 2); N (1791 ed. with second state of pls. 1 and 2); P (1791 ed. with second state of pls. 1 and 2); R (1791 ed. with first state of the pls., loose pls. from the 1796 ed., and loose pls. 1 in the first state and 2-6 in the second state); RNE (1791 ed. with second state of pls. 1 and 2); UCLA (1791 ed. with first state of the pls.); UW (1791 ed. with second state of pls. 1 and 2).
COPY REPRODUCED: P (1791 ed. with second state of pls. 1 and 2 and first state of pls. 3-6).
Russell #7; Keynes #69; Binyon #12-17; Bentley & Nurmi #421A-B.

IV. Edward Young: NIGHT THOUGHTS, 1797.

TITLE-PAGE:
THE COMPLAINT, | AND | THE CONSOLATION; | OR, | NIGHT THOUGHTS, | BY | EDWARD YOUNG, LL.D. | [double rule] | ————*fatis contraria fata rependens.* | [to the right] VIRG. | [double rule] | LONDON: | PRINTED BY R. NOBLE, | FOR R. EDWARDS, No. 142, BOND-STREET, | M DCC XCVII.

> NOTE: In 18 of the copies examined the printed title-page was printed on J. Whatman paper matching that upon which the engravings are printed. One copy however, the Doheny copy, has the title-page printed on laid paper with a greenish cast bearing a watermark which we have been unable to trace. The watermark bears a fleur-de-lis and shield with the initials C over GVL. The title-page in the Doheny copy is identical in every other way to the rest of the copies examined, and no explanation can be given for its variance.

COLLATION: No signatures. 56 leaves with 43 plates printed on 36 leaves. 42.2 × 33 cm.

> NOTE: In the rare prospectus for *Night Thoughts*, reprinted in Keynes, p. 202, we are told that the volume is to be an "atlas sized quarto." According to Labarre's *Dictionary and Encyclopedia of Paper and Paper-making* (Amsterdam, 1952) the atlas-sized sheet is usually 34 inches in length by 26 inches in width. In a quarto format this size sheet produces exactly the 17 by 13 inch leaves found in uncut copies of the volume. And, though the usual indices of format—conjugacy, watermarks—are in this instance unreliable, as will be explained later, the evidence of the prospectus permits us to determine with confidence a quarto format.
>
> The manner in which the book was printed is, however, a considerable puzzle. First, all the leaves appear to be disjunct with two exceptions. The Newberry's copy of *Night Thoughts* is one of the few uncut copies loosely bound. Usually the collector has had his prized volume tightly and handsomely bound, which effectively forbids the bibliographer's inspection of conjugacy. The decaying spine of the Newberry's copy, however, shows us that pp. v-vi & vii-viii are conjugate. The Bodleian Library, Oxford, informs us that they have a copy of *Night Thoughts* in the original boards, incomplete, in which they can determine that the title-leaf and the first leaf of the Advertisement are also conjugate. The Newberry copy clearly does not show this conjugacy, however, and the Doheny copy, with the unusual title-page paper, also would seem to disagree.
>
> While the evidence of the watermarks provides no positive identification of the format, the irregularity of their appearance may tell us something of the printing process. Apparently, the text panels were printed on 12½ atlas sheets of J. Whatman 1794 paper. One sheet without text panels could have been used to print the four engraved title-pages so that the entire book requires 13½ sheets for printing. After the text panels were printed in a quarto format upon the sheet, all those leaves which were to bear plates were cut away. The absence of conjugacy can only be explained by the necessity of imposing the plates on quarter sheets. Apparently the engraved plate was positioned in the rolling press so that the text panel, already printed on the page, would finally appear within the space Blake left for it in his design. In those plates in which the lower edge of the design seems to run off the bottom of the page, the print-

er has apparently failed to judge correctly the position of the text panel within Blake's design. These plates wherein the bottom of the design extends below the bottom of the page normally appear with an unusually large top margin, suggesting that there would have been plenty of space for the plate to appear fully on the page if the text panel had been properly positioned.

In all copies examined, the absence of conjugacy is further indicated by the great irregularity in the number and position of watermarks in each copy. The watermarks, for example, only appear nine times in the Bancroft Library, Berkeley, copy, and twenty times in the uncut RNE copy.

PAGINATION: [i-iii] iv-viii [ix-xii] 1-16 [17-18] 19-42 [43-44] 45-63 [64-66] 67--95 [96].

CONTENTS: p. [i] title-page. p. [ii] *blank*. p. [iii] Advertisement. p. [ix] Explanation of the Engravings. p. [xi] engraved title-page. p. [xii] *blank*. p. 1 Night the First. p. [17] engraved title-page. p. [18] *blank*. p. 19 Night the Second. p. [43] engraved title-page. p. [44] *blank*. p. 45 Night the Third. p. [64] *blank*. p. [65] engraved title-page. p. [66] *blank*. p. 67 Night the Fourth. p. [96] *blank*.

NOTE: The Explanation of the Engravings, described here as pp. [ix-x] and quoted in the descriptions of the plates, is occasionally found at the end of the book, after p. [96].

PLATES

Forty-three intaglio copper-plate engravings printed on text and title pages, all designed and engraved by Blake. All but pls. 1-3, 6, 8, 11, and 34 are signed with Blake's monogram "*WB*" and some form of "*inv. & sc.*" in a semi-circle above the initials as listed for each pl. below. Plate size varies slightly, and in most cases is no more than a few cm. larger on the left, right, and bottom margins than the design sizes listed herein. The text panels range between 23 × 15.5 cm. and 24 × 17.2 cm. Even in uncut copies the imprint and margins of some designs do not appear, because plates were quite frequently positioned improperly relative to the page in printing. Many designs were engraved without a definite lower border, and therefore the positions of the imprints listed here are given as the distance from the lower margin of the text panel to the imprint.

There are twenty-four proofs without text in the collection of Mr. Philip Hofer, as listed in Bentley & Nurmi, p. 169. Blake also used forty-seven *Night Thoughts* proofs without text on which to write part of his *Vala* manuscript. These are recorded and reproduced in William Blake, *Vala or the Four Zoas*, ed. G. E. Bentley, Jr. (Oxford, 1963). Among these pulls are two distinct proof states for some of the designs. The differences between the *Vala* proofs and the published states are noted for each pl. below. See also the notes below following pls. 5 and and 25 for more information on early states. For a discussion and list of colored copies see W. E. Moss, "The Coloured Copies of Blake's 'Night Thoughts,'" *Blake Newsletter*, 2, No. 2 (Sept. 15, 1968), 19-23 and G. E. Bentley, Jr., "A Census of Coloured Copies of Young's *Night Thoughts* (1797)," *Blake Newsletter*, 2, No. 3 (Dec. 15, 1968), 41-45. See also Bentley, *The Blake Collection of Mrs. Landon K. Thorne* (New York, 1971), footnote on p. 57, for a correction.

All but pages 15, 41, 49, 54, and 75 of those surrounded by an engraving have one line of text, as given below, which is preceded by an asterisk to indicate the subject of the illustration. Two unillustrated pages, 20 and 61, also have lines preceded by an asterisk—see the notes following pls. 12 and 29 below for details.

The 537 *Night Thoughts* water color drawings in the BM Department of Prints and Drawings include the preliminary designs for all the engravings. Except for the title-page to Night the Fourth, the water color preliminaries appear in the same Night, but not on the same page number (as noted for each design below) as the engraved designs, because each Night is separately paginated in the water colors and the edition of the text used with the water colors is not the same as the one accompanying the engravings. In a few cases, also noted below, the line marked for illustration in the water colors differs from that in the engravings. The responsibility for the asterisks in the engravings and the pencil markings in the water colors has never been conclusively determined. The "Explanation of the Engravings," recorded below for each plate ("Explanation"), is very tentatively attributed to Fuseli in Alexander Gilchrist, *Life of William Blake* (London & Cambridge, 1863), I, 139-40.

1. Unnumbered and uncounted title-page: *NIGHT the FIRST,* | ON | LIFE, | DEATH | AND | IMMORTALITY.
   MONOGRAM INSCRIPTION: none.
   IMPRINT lower left: *Pub.d June 27th 1796, by R. Edwards, No. 142 New Bond Street.*
   DESIGN SIZE: 39 × 32.5 cm. The imprint is 11.7 cm. below the text panel.
   EXPLANATION: Frontispiece to Night the First. Death, in the character of an old man, having swept away with one hand part of the family seen in this print, is presenting with the other their spirits to immortality.
   NOTE: The pl. appears as p. 140 of the *Vala* manuscript where it is trimmed on the top, bottom, and left margins, but is otherwise the same as the published state. The design appears on the title-page to Night the First in the water colors.

2. P. 1.
   LINE ILLUSTRATED: *Swift on his downy pinion flies from woe,
   MONOGRAM INSCRIPTION: none.
   IMPRINT lower left: as on pl. 1.
   DESIGN SIZE: 37.7 × 32 cm. The imprint is 11.4 cm. below the text panel.
   EXPLANATION: Sleep forsaking the couch of care, sheds his influence, by the touch of his magic wand, on the shepherd's flock.
   NOTE: The pl. does not appear in the *Vala* manuscript. No line marked for illustration in the water colors, p. [3].

3. P. 4.
   LINE ILLUSTRATED: *What, though my soul fantastick measures trod
   MONOGRAM INSCRIPTION: none.
   IMPRINT lower left: *Pub.d June. 27th 1796, by R. Edwards, No. 142 New Bond Street.*
   DESIGN SIZE: 37 × 32 cm. The imprint is 9.4 cm. below the text panel.
   EXPLANATION: The imagery of dreaming variously delineated according to the poet's description in the passage referred to by the *.

NOTE: The proof on p. 107 of the *Vala* manuscript contains grass rather than crosshatching just above the sleeping figure's head. This proof is trimmed at the bottom, thus cutting off any imprint if present. No line marked for illustration in the water colors, p. 9.

4. P. 7, recto of pl. 5.

    LINE ILLUSTRATED: *Till at Death's toll, whose restless iron tongue
    MONOGRAM INSCRIPTION, lower left margin: *WB inv. & sc*
    IMPRINT lower left: *Pubd June, 27, 1796, by R. Edwards, No 142 New Bond Street*
    DESIGN SIZE: 34.9 (top of the text panel to lowest engraved line) × 29.5 cm. The imprint is 12 cm. below the text panel.
    EXPLANATION: Death, tolling a bell, summonses a person from sleep to his kingdom the grave.

    NOTE: Proofs appear as pp. 53 and 71 of the *Vala* manuscript, both without imprint and lacking the shading behind the figure with a bell. No line is marked for illustration in the water colors, p. 13.

5. P. 8, verso of pl. 4.

    LINE ILLUSTRATED: *Death! great proprietor of all! 'tis thine
    MONOGRAM INSCRIPTION, bottom of left margin: *WB inv & sc*
    IMPRINT lower left: *Pubd June, 27, 1796, by R. Edwards, 142 New Bond Street.*
    DESIGN SIZE: 39.7 × 32.2 cm. The imprint is 10.8 cm. below the text panel.
    EXPLANATION: The universal empire of Death characterized by his plucking the sun from his sphere.

    NOTE: In an uncut RNE copy, with the lower plate-mark clearly showing, the imprint does not appear. Although the design itself is the same as in imprinted copies, this may be an early state. See also pl. 25 below. The proof on p. 81 of the *Vala* manuscript lacks shading along the left margin, on the faces and hair of all three figures, on the left arm and beard of the standing figure, and on the mustache of the lower right head. The proof on p. 133 is a later state, lacking only a few lines in the hair and mustache of the lower right head. Both proofs lack the monogram and imprint. No line marked for illustration in the water colors, p. 15.

6. P. 10.

    LINE ILLUSTRATED: * Disease invades the chastest temperance,
    MONOGRAM INSCRIPTION: none.
    IMPRINT lower left: as on pl. 1.
    DESIGN SIZE: 38.4 × 32.5 cm. The imprint is 11.4 cm. below the text panel.
    EXPLANATION: An evil genius holding two phials, from one pours disease into the ear of a shepherd, and from the other scatters a blight among his flock; intimating that no condition is exempt from affliction.

    NOTE: This pl. does not appear in the *Vala* manuscript. No line marked for illustration in the water colors, p. 19.

7. P. 12.

    LINE ILLUSTRATED: *Its favours here are trials, not rewards;
    MONOGRAM INSCRIPTION, lower left margin: *WB inv.*

IMPRINT: In the proof of this pl., used for p. 77 of the *Vala* manuscript, the imprint reads as on pl. 1, and it is very likely that this was retained in the published state. Among the nineteen copies examined, however, only the UCLA copy has the plate printed high enough on the page to show any evidence of the imprint. Only the top half of the imprint appears in the UCLA copy, and therefore it can generally confirm the imprint on the *Vala* proof but does not provide information on the exact punctuation.

DESIGN SIZE: 38.2 × 31.8 cm. In the *Vala* manuscript, p. 77, the imprint is 12.4 cm. below the text panel.

EXPLANATION: The frailty of the blessings of this life demonstrated, by a representation in which the happiness of a little family is suddenly destroyed by the accident of the husband's death from the bite of a serpent.

NOTE: The proof on p. 77 of the *Vala* manuscript lacks the birds to the left of the text panel, the vine and bird at the top of the text panel, much of the shading on the figures and landscape, and all of the shading in the sky. The land on the right extends further up the plate. The proof on p. 49 is a later state lacking the vine and the largest bird to the left of the text panel; the shading is the same as in the published state. The imprint has been rubbed out up to "N?" with only a slight trace remaining. The monogram is absent from both proofs. No line marked for illustration in the water colors, p. 22.

8. P. 13.

LINE ILLUSTRATED: *The present moment terminates our sight;

MONOGRAM INSCRIPTION: none.

IMPRINT lower left: as on pl. 1.

DESIGN SIZE: 37 × 29.7 cm. The imprint is 11.2 cm. below the text panel.

EXPLANATION: The insecurity of life exemplified by the figure of Death menacing with his dart, and doubtful which he shall strike; the mother, or the infant at her breast.

NOTE: The proof on p. 101 of the *Vala* manuscript lacks some shading on the lower part of the pillow and on the child's left foot, but the pillow has a button not retained in the published state. The pl. is trimmed at the top, cutting off the descending figure's toes, and at the bottom, cutting off the imprint if present. No line marked for illustration in the water colors, p. 26.

9. P. 15, recto of pl. 10.

LINE ILLUSTRATED: *The longest night though longer far, would fail,

MONOGRAM INSCRIPTION, bottom left margin: *WB inv & sc.*

IMPRINT lower left: *Pubd June 27. 1796, by R: Edwards, No 142, New Bond Street.*

DESIGN SIZE: 35.6 × 26.3 cm. The imprint is 10.5 cm. below the text panel.

EXPLANATION: The author encircled by thorns, emblematical of grief, lamenting the loss of his friend to the midnight hours.

NOTE: The proof on p. 91 of the *Vala* manuscript lacks the imprint and some shading on the supine figure's foot and on the thorny vine around his lower body. No line marked for illustration in the water colors, p. 29.

10. P. 16, verso of pl. 9.

LINE ILLUSTRATED: *Oft bursts my song beyond the bounds of life;

MONOGRAM INSCRIPTION, lower right between two thorny branches: *WB inv. & sc.*

IMPRINT lower left: London, *Pub.ᵈ June 21, 1796, by R. Edwards, 142 New Bond Street.*

DESIGN SIZE: 38.1 × 30.5 cm. The imprint is 9.8 cm. below the text panel.

EXPLANATION: The struggling of the soul for immortality, represented by a figure holding a lyre and springing into the air, but confined by a chain to the earth.

> NOTE: The proof on p. 123 of the *Vala* manuscript lacks the imprint and some of the shading on the figure's right arm and hand. No line marked for illustration in the water colors, p. 30.

11. P. [17], title-page: NIGHT *the* SECOND | ON | TIME, | DEATH | AND | FRIENDSHIP.

MONOGRAM INSCRIPTION: none.

IMPRINT lower left: as on pl. 1.

DESIGN SIZE: 39.2 × 32.8 cm. The imprint is 9.8 cm. below the text panel.

EXPLANATION: Frontispiece to Night the Second. Time endeavouring to avert the arrow of Death from two friends.

> NOTE: The pl. does not appear in the *Vala* manuscript. The design appears on the title-page to Night the Second in the water colors.

12. P. 19.

LINE ILLUSTRATED: *Emblem of that which shall awake the dead,

MONOGRAM INSCRIPTION, lower left over skeleton's shroud: *WB inv. & sc*

IMPRINT lower left: *Pub.ᵈ June, 27, 1796, by R. Edwards, N.º 142 New Bond Street.*

DESIGN SIZE: 34.2 × 31.3 cm. The imprint is 10.2 cm. below the text panel.

EXPLANATION: A skeleton discovering the first symptoms of re-animation on the sounding of the archangel's trump.

> NOTE: The proof on p. 105 of the *Vala* manuscript lacks the imprint and some shading on the descending figure's legs and on the skull. In the water colors, p. [5], the same line quoted above is marked for illustration.
>
> On p. 20 in the 1797 text the sixth line, "I know thou say'st it: says thy life the same?" is preceded by an asterisk. It is likely that the design on p. 6 of the water colors, on which this same line is marked for illustration, was originally intended to be included among the engraved designs and, when excluded, the asterisk was overlooked and not removed.

13. P. 23, recto of pl. 14.

LINE ILLUSTRATED: *We censure nature for a span too short;

MONOGRAM INSCRIPTION, lower right above and to the left of the first word of the imprint: *WB inv. & sc*

IMPRINT lower right: *Pub.ᵈ June 27ᵗʰ 1796 by R. Edwards N.º 142 New Bond Street.*

DESIGN SIZE: 36.6 × 28.4 cm. The imprint is 10.1 cm. below the text panel.

EXPLANATION: A man measuring an infant with his span, in allusion to the shortness of life.

NOTE: The pl. on p. 63 of the *Vala* manuscript is the same as the published state. In the water color designs, p. 11, two non-consecutive lines are marked for illustration, "Who murders Time, He crushes in the Birth" and "Like Children babbling nonsense in their sports,"

14. P. 24, verso of pl. 13.
    LINE ILLUSTRATED: *Time, in advance, behind him hides his wings,
    MONOGRAM INSCRIPTION, lower right margin: *WB inv*
    IMPRINT lower left: as on pl. 13.
    DESIGN SIZE: 37.7 × 31.9 cm. The imprint is 9.7 cm. below the text panel.
    EXPLANATION: Our inattention to the progress of Time illustrated by a figure of the *god*, (as he is called by the poet) creeping towards us with stealthy pace, and carefully concealing his wings from our view.
    NOTE: The proof on p. 99 of the *Vala* manuscript lacks the monogram, the parallel lines above the text panel indicating sky, the veins on the large figure's left arm, and much of the shading on the large figure's arms, legs, and wings beneath his legs and at the right. The face of the small figure leaning on the hourglass is in a slightly different position. In the water colors, p. 12, the same line quoted above is marked for illustration.

15. P. 25, recto of pl. 16.
    LINE ILLUSTRATED: none marked.
    MONOGRAM INSCRIPTION, lower left, 4.5 cm. in from the left margin: *WB inv & sc*
    IMPRINT lower left: *Pubd. June 27. 1796, by Rt Edwards, No. 142 New Bond Street.*
    DESIGN SIZE: 39.7 × 33 cm. The imprint is 11.3 cm. below the text panel.
    EXPLANATION: Time having passed us, is seen displaying his "broad pinions," and treading nearly on the summit of the globe, eager "to join anew Eternity his sire."
    NOTE: The pl. on p. 127 of the *Vala* manuscript is the same as the published state. In the water color designs, p. 13, "Behold him, when past by; what then is seen," is the line marked for illustration. This line is printed on p. 24 in the 1797 text.

16. P. 26, verso of pl. 15.
    LINE ILLUSTRATED: *Measuring his motions by revolving spheres;
    MONOGRAM INSCRIPTION, lower right margin: *WB inv & sc*
    IMPRINT: In the proof of this pl. used for p. 135 of the *Vala* manuscript, the imprint reads "*Pubd. June 27. 1796, by R. Edwards, No. 142 New Bond Street.*" It is very likely that this imprint was retained in the published state, but this could not be confirmed by any of the nineteen copies examined, all of which are cropped or have the plate printed too low on the page for any imprint to show.
    DESIGN SIZE: 37.4 × 32.8 cm. In the *Vala* manuscript, p. 135, the imprint is 13.5 cm. below the text panel.
    EXPLANATION: The same power [time] in his character of destroyer, mowing down indiscriminately the frail inhabitants of this world.

NOTE: The proof on p. 135 of the *Vala* manuscript lacks some shading on the large figure's right calf and on all the small figures. The faces of the corpses are undeveloped and the expressions of the mother with a baby in her arms and the girl by the scythe are slightly different. In the water colors, p. 16, the same line quoted above is marked for illustration.

17. P. 27.
    LINE ILLUSTRATED: *O treacherous conscience! while she seems to sleep
    MONOGRAM INSCRIPTION, lower right margin: *WB inv & sc*
    IMPRINT lower left: as on pl. 9.
    DESIGN SIZE: 35.4 × 29.5 cm. The imprint is 11.6 cm. below the text panel.
    EXPLANATION: Conscience represented as a recording angel; who is veiled, and in the act of noting down the sin of intemperance in a bacchanalian.
    NOTE: The proof on p. 103 of the *Vala* manuscript lacks the monogram but is otherwise the same as the published state. No line marked for illustration in the water colors, p. 19.

18. P. 31.
    LINE ILLUSTRATED: *'Tis greatly wise to talk with our past hours,
    MONOGRAM INSCRIPTION, lower right margin: *WB inv & sc*
    IMPRINT lower left: *Pub?d June, 27th 1796, by R. Edwards, No 142 New Bond Street.*
    DESIGN SIZE: 35.7 (top of text panel to bottom of monogram) × 32.4 cm. The imprint is 11.7 cm. below the text panel.
    EXPLANATION: A good man conversing with his past hours, and examining their report. The hours are drawn as aërial and shadowy beings, some of whom are bringing their scrolls to the inquirer, while others are carrying their record to heaven.
    NOTE: The pl. on p. 125 of the *Vala* manuscript is the same as the published state, except that it has been trimmed on the bottom at a point which might have cut off the imprint if present. In the water colors, p. 25, the same line quoted above is marked for illustration.

19. P. 33.
    LINE ILLUSTRATED: *Like that, the dial speaks; and points to thee,
    MONOGRAM INSCRIPTION, lower right beneath the cloud: *WB inv & sc*
    IMPRINT lower left: as on pl. 1.
    DESIGN SIZE: 36.8 × 30 cm. The imprint is 11.8 cm. below the text panel.
    EXPLANATION: Belshazzar terrified in the midst of his impious debauch by the hand-writing on the wall. The passage marked out by the asterisk, sufficiently explains the propriety with which the story is alluded to by the poet, and delineated by the artist.
    NOTE: The pl. on p. 51 of the *Vala* manuscript lacks the monogram, some shading at the lower left corner of the text panel, and some shading below the right figure's left arm and on his right shoulder. No line marked for illustration in the water colors, p. 27.

20. P. 35.
    LINE ILLUSTRATED: *Teaching, we learn; and giving, we retain
    MONOGRAM INSCRIPTION, lower left margin: *WB inv. s*

IMPRINT lower left: *Pubd June, 27th 1796, by R. Edwards. No 142. New Bond Street.*
DESIGN SIZE: 38.6 × 32.2 cm. The imprint is 12 cm. below the text panel.
EXPLANATION: A parent communicating instruction to his family.
    NOTE: The proof on p. 95 of the *Vala* manuscript lacks the cloak on the harper above the text panel, a few lines in his hair, and the lock of hair falling beneath his neck. In the water color designs, p. 31, the line marked for illustration is "*Speech ventilates our intellectual fire;*"

21. P. 37.
LINE ILLUSTRATED: *Love, and love only, is the loan for love.
MONOGRAM INSCRIPTION, lower right margin: *WB inv: & sc*
IMPRINT: none.
DESIGN SIZE: 38.8 × 30.8 cm.
EXPLANATION: The story of the good Samaritan, introduced by the artist as an illustration of the poet's sentiment, that love alone and kind offices can purchase love.
    NOTE: The proof on p. 129 of the *Vala* manuscript lacks some shading on the stooping figure's neck and clothing. In the water colors, p. 35, the same line quoted above is marked for illustration.

22. P. 40.
LINE ILLUSTRATED: *Angels should paint it, angels ever there;
MONOGRAM INSCRIPTION, lower left margin: *WB inv & s.*
IMPRINT lower left: *London, Pubd Jan: 4, 1797, by R. Edwards. 142 New Bond Street.*
DESIGN SIZE: 35.1 × 31.2 cm. The imprint is 10 cm. below the text panel.
EXPLANATION: Angels attending the death-bed of the righteous, and administering consolation to his last moments.
    NOTE: The proof on p. 131 of the *Vala* manuscript lacks the monogram and imprint, the vertical lines on the scroll-bed and the horizontal lines beneath it, and some shading on all four faces as well as on the robes of the figures. The proof on p. 121 is a later state, lacking the imprint and the shading noted above for p. 131.

23. P. 41.
LINE ILLUSTRATED: none marked.
MONOGRAM INSCRIPTION, left of the text panel at the seventh line from the bottom: *WB inv & sc*
IMPRINT lower right: *London: Pub. Mar. 22, 1797, by R. Edwards, 142 New Bond Street.*
DESIGN SIZE: 40 × 29.8 cm. The imprint is 12.1 cm. below the text panel.
EXPLANATION: Angels conveying the spirit of the good man to heaven.
    NOTE: The proof on p. 117 of the *Vala* manuscript lacks the imprint but is otherwise the same as the published state. In the water color designs, p. 43, the line marked for illustration is "One radiant Mark; the Deathbed of the Just:" This is one of the concluding lines to "Night the Second" in the edition used with the water colors not printed in the 1797 text.

24. P. [43], Title-page: NIGHT | THE | THIRD, | NARCISSA.

MONOGRAM INSCRIPTION, bottom right beneath the object on which the female figure stands: *WB inv & s*
IMPRINT: none.
DESIGN SIZE: 40.5 × 32.5 cm.
EXPLANATION: Frontispiece to Night the Third. A female figure, who appears from the crescent beneath her feet to have surmounted the trials of this world, is admitted to an eternity of glory: eternity is represented by its usual emblem —a serpent with its extremities united.
NOTE: The pl. on p. 73 of the *Vala* manuscript lacks the engraved title within the text panel, but otherwise is the same as the published state. The design appears on the title-page to Night the Third in the water colors.

25. P. 46.
LINE ILLUSTRATED: *Where sense runs savage broke from reason's chain,
MONOGRAM INSCRIPTION, lower right margin: *WB inv & s*
IMPRINT lower left: *London, Pub.d Jan: 1, 1797, by R. Edwards, 142 New Bond St.t*
DESIGN SIZE: 38.5 × 31.3 cm. The imprint is 10.6 cm. below the text panel.
EXPLANATION: The folly and danger of pursuing the pleasures of sense as the chief objects of life illustrated by the figure of Death just ready to throw his pall over a young and wanton female.
NOTE: In an uncut RNE copy and in the University of Illinois Copy, with the lower plate-mark clearly showing, the imprint does not appear. Although the design itself is the same as in imprinted copies, this may be an early state. See also pl. 5 above. The pl. does not appear in the *Vala* manuscript. No line marked for illustration in the water colors, p. 6.

26. P. 49.
LINE ILLUSTRATED: none marked.
MONOGRAM INSCRIPTION, lower right margin: *WB inv & s*
IMPRINT lower left: *London, Pub.d June 27. 1796, by R Edwards, 142 New Bond Str.t*
DESIGN SIZE: 40.4 × 32.1 cm. The imprint is 11.2 cm. below the text panel.
EXPLANATION: The author supporting a female figure, and presenting her to the sun; whose aid he seems to solicit, and whose chariot is seen above, surrounded and in some measure obscured by clouds. The artist refers to the circumstance alluded to in the poem, of the author's having attended his step-daughter (Narcissa) who was languishing in a decline, to a more southern clime.
NOTE: The proof on p. 47 of the *Vala* manuscript lacks the imprint and monogram, but is otherwise the same as the published state. No line marked for illustration in the water colors, p. 12.

27. P. 54.
LINE ILLUSTRATED, marked with an asterisk on p. 53: *The vale of death! that hush'd cimmerian vale,
MONOGRAM INSCRIPTION, lower left margin: *WB inv & s*
IMPRINT lower right: *London: Pub. Mar. 22. 1797, by R. Edwards, 142, New Bond Street.*

22

DESIGN SIZE: 38.1 × 31.1 cm. The imprint is 9 cm. below the text panel.

EXPLANATION: The vale of death, where the Power of darkness broods over his victims, as they are borne down to the grave by the torrent of a sinful life.

NOTE: The proof on p. 83 of the *Vala* manuscript lacks the imprint and shading on the bearded swimmer's face and cowl and on the extended arms of the female seen quarter-face. Some of the lines defining the hair of the swimmer with his face down in the water and hands in prayer are also absent. In the water colors, p. 19, the same line quoted above is marked for illustration.

28. P. 55.

LINE ILLUSTRATED: *Ungrateful, shall we grieve their hovering shades

MONOGRAM INSCRIPTION, left of the last line of text: *WB inv. & s.*

IMPRINT: none.

DESIGN SIZE: 35.1 (top of text panel to lowest engraved line) × 30.4 cm.

EXPLANATION: His guardian angel sent to reprove a mourner for his improper indulgence of sorrow on the tomb of his friend: with one hand the angel touches the object of his errand, and with the other points to those realms of light in which the deceased was at rest from his labours.

NOTE: The proof on p. 79 of the *Vala* manuscript lacks some shading on the tombstone and has been trimmed at the bottom, cutting off the grave mound and the seated figure from the waist down. In the water color designs, p. 21, the line marked for illustration is "Are Angels sent on Errands full of Love:"

29. P. 57.

LINE ILLUSTRATED: *Trembling each gulp, lest death should snatch the bowl.

MONOGRAM INSCRIPTION, lower right margin: *WB inv & s*

IMPRINT: none.

DESIGN SIZE: 38 (along engraved line on left margin) × 30.6 cm.

EXPLANATION: Death with his uplifted dart just disclosing himself to a party of bacchanals; one of whom still continues his intoxicating draught, while his comrades discover symptoms of extreme alarm on the unexpected intrusion of so welcome a guest.

NOTE: The pl. on p. 93 of the *Vala* manuscript lacks only some shading on the upper left. In the water color designs, p. 24, the line marked for illustration is "Still-streaming Thoroughfares of dull Debauch!"

On p. 61 in the 1797 text the seventh line from the bottom, "Age and disease; disease, though long my guest" is preceded by an asterisk. It is likely that the design on p. 32 of the water colors, on which the same line is marked for illustration, was originally intended to be included among the engraved designs and, when excluded, the asterisk was overlooked and not removed.

30. P. 63.

LINE ILLUSTRATED: *This KING OF TERRORS is the PRINCE OF PEACE."

MONOGRAM INSCRIPTION, lower left margin: *WB inv & sc*

IMPRINT: none.

DESIGN SIZE: 38.2 × 30.9 cm.

EXPLANATION: To the eye of the righteous the countenance of the King of Terrors is changed into that of the Prince of Peace.

NOTE: The pl. on p. 43 of the *Vala* manuscript is the same as the published state. In the water color designs, p. 33, "Death, the great Counsellor, who Man inspires" is the line marked for illustration. This line is printed on p. 62 in the 1797 text.

31. P. [65], Title-page to "Night the Fourth": THE | CHRISTIAN | TRIUMPH.
    MONOGRAM INSCRIPTION, left margin to the left of "CHRISTIAN": *WB in & s*
    IMPRINT lower left: *Pub^d June 1st 1797 by R. Edwards New Bond Street*
    DESIGN SIZE: 38 × 31.2 cm. The imprint is 19.6 cm. below the "*T*" of "*TRI-UMPH.*"
    EXPLANATION: Frontispiece to Night the Fourth. The resurrection of our Saviour, typical of the resurrection of all his servants from the grave.
    NOTE: The proof on p. 114 of the *Vala* manuscript lacks the engraved title inscription, the imprint, and some shading on the left figure's face and neck, and the top figure's left eyebrow. This is the first design in the water color series.

32. P. 70.
    LINE ILLUSTRATED: *Till death, that mighty hunter, earths them all.
    MONOGRAM INSCRIPTION, lower right margin: *WB inv & sc.*
    IMPRINT lower left: *London, Pub^d June 27. 1796. by R Edwards, 142 New Bond Street.*
    DESIGN SIZE: 39.5 × 31.3 cm. The imprint is 12.3 cm. below the text panel.
    EXPLANATION: Death, as a huntsman, pursuing with ferocious pleasure his human game.
    NOTE: The proof on p. 57 of the *Vala* manuscript lacks the imprint but otherwise is the same as the published state. In the water colors, p. 8, the same line quoted above is marked for illustration. A pencil sketch of the design usually entitled "Let Loose the Dogs of War," now in the Nelson Gallery-Atkins Museum, Kansas City, Missouri, is reproduced in *Studio*, 146 (1953), 59 and in *Imagination and Vision: Prints and Drawings of William Blake*, Miscellaneous Publications of the [Kansas] Museum of Art, No. 84 (n.p., [1971]), fig. 1.

33. P. 72.
    LINE ILLUSTRATED: *And vapid; sense and reason shew the door,
    MONOGRAM INSCRIPTION, lower left margin: *WB in & s*
    IMPRINT lower left: *Pub^d June 1st 1797, by R. Edwards, N° 142 New Bond Street.*
    DESIGN SIZE: 38.3 × 31.4 cm. The imprint is 11.5 cm. below the text panel.
    EXPLANATION: Two figures, intended to represent Sense and Reason, pointing to another scene of things, and admonishing the author that it is time for him to depart from the present.
    NOTE: The proof on p. 67 of the *Vala* manuscript lacks the imprint and some shading on the face and right hand of the right figure. In the water colors, p. 10, the same line quoted above is marked for illustration.

34. P. 73.
    LINE ILLUSTRATED: *Draw the dire steel?—ah no!—the dreadful blessing
    MONOGRAM INSCRIPTION: none.
    IMPRINT: none.

DESIGN SIZE: 38.3 × 29.5 cm.

EXPLANATION: The Saviour represented in the furnace of affliction, and agonized with torture for the sins of the human race.

>NOTE: In the proof on p. 111 of the *Vala* manuscript the figure's head is given in profile (three-quarter face in the published state) and the shading on the gown lower left extends about 3 cm. along the border of the text panel. This shading was eliminated in the published state, because the text panel was widened about .5 cm. on the left margin. This proof lacks the heavy shading on the fire to the right and left and some shading on the figure's neck, but has a monogram inscription on the lower left margin ("*WB inv & s*"). This monogram does not appear in the published state, except for a small part of the arc extending from the "*B*," because the design was cut down about 1.7 cm. on the left margin before publication. The proofs on pp. 59 and 115 have the monogram and shading on the gown as described for p. 111 above, but are otherwise the same as the published state. In the water colors, p. 12, the same line quoted above is marked for illustration.

35. P. 75.

LINE ILLUSTRATED: none marked.

MONOGRAM INSCRIPTION, bottom left 5.3 cm. from the left margin: *WB in. & s*

IMPRINT: none.

DESIGN SIZE: 37.4 × 31.2 cm.

EXPLANATION: The sun as described by the poet, averting his face (which he hides also with his hands) from the shocking spectacle of our Lord's sufferings.

>NOTE: The pl. appearing on p. 75 of the *Vala* manuscript is the same as the published state. In the water color designs, p. 16, two non-consecutive lines are marked for illustration, "The Sun beheld it—No, the shocking Scene" and "*Sun*! didst thou fly thy Maker's Pain? or start"

36. P. 80.

LINE ILLUSTRATED: *The thunder, if in that the ALMIGHTY dwells?

MONOGRAM INSCRIPTION, lower left margin within the design: *WB in & s*

IMPRINT lower left: as on pl. 33.

DESIGN SIZE: 36.4 × 31.4 cm. The imprint is 7.9 cm. below the text panel.

EXPLANATION: A personification of Thunder directing the adoration of the poet to the Almighty in heaven.

>NOTE: The proof on p. 65 of the *Vala* manuscript lacks the imprint but is otherwise the same as the published state. In the water colors, p. 24, the same line quoted above is marked for illustration.

37. P. 86.

LINE ILLUSTRATED: *His hand the good man fastens on the skies,

MONOGRAM INSCRIPTION, to the right of the bottom right corner of the text panel: *WB in. & s*

IMPRINT: none.

DESIGN SIZE: 36.8 × 30.6 cm.

EXPLANATION: The exalted views of a good man beyond the pleasures of this life, allegorically described by a figure in the clouds, with one hand fixed in the sky, and with the other pointing to the earth beneath him.
NOTE: In the proof on p. 61 of the *Vala* manuscript the figure's foot can be seen below the text panel which at its base is about 8 mm. less in width than in the published state. This proof lacks some of the lines defining the figure's hair and the shading on his right arm and left eyebrow. The proof on p. 119 is a slightly later state, showing a few more lines in the figure's hair. In the water colors, p. 32, the same line quoted above is marked for illustration.

38. P. 87, recto of pl. 39.
LINE ILLUSTRATED: *Is lost in love! thou great PHILANTHROPIST!
MONOGRAM INSCRIPTION, lower left margin: *WB in & s*
IMPRINT: none.
DESIGN SIZE: 34.6 × 31.5 cm.
EXPLANATION: Christ represented as the great philanthropist, receiving and instructing all ages and sexes.
NOTE: The proof on p. 55 of the *Vala* manuscript lacks the thin line of shading to the left of the tallest figure's right arm. The width of the text panel is 1.5 cm. less than in the published state. In the water color designs, p. 34, the same line quoted above is marked for illustration.

39. P. 88, verso of pl. 38.
LINE ILLUSTRATED: *But for the blessing wrestle not with heaven!
MONOGRAM INSCRIPTION, right of the text panel at the fourteenth line of the text: *WB in & s*
IMPRINT lower margin: *Pub.d June 1st 1797, by R. Edwards, No 142 New Bond Street*
DESIGN SIZE: 34.4 (top of text panel to lowest engraved line) × 29.3 cm. The imprint is 10.7 cm. below the text panel.
EXPLANATION (incorrectly labeled as the explanation of p. 89, which in fact has no design): Earnest prayer and intercourse with Heaven compared to the wrestling of Jacob with the angel for a blessing.
NOTE: The proof on p. 137 of the *Vala* manuscript lacks the imprint but is otherwise the same as the published state. The part of the figures covered by the text panel has been drawn in with pencil in this proof. In the water colors, p. 36, the same line quoted above is marked for illustration.

40. P. 90.
LINE ILLUSTRATED: *That touch, with charm celestial heals the soul
MONOGRAM INSCRIPTION, right of the text panel at the fifth line of text from the bottom: *WB in. & s*
IMPRINT: none.
DESIGN SIZE: 37.1 × 29.6 cm.
EXPLANATION: The Saviour healing Affliction by a touch with his hand
NOTE: The proofs on p. 45 and 97 of the *Vala* manuscript lack the butterfly and cocoon above the text panel, some lines defining the hair of both figures, and some shading on the upper figure's face, beard, neck, and forehead, and on the lower figure's face, right arm, and left thigh. In the water colors, p. 39, the same line quoted above is marked for illustration.

41. P. 92.
: LINE ILLUSTRATED: *When faith is virtue, reason makes it so.
: MONOGRAM INSCRIPTION, 2.1 cm. below the bottom margin of the text panel at the last word in the text: *WB in & s*
: IMPRINT: none.
: DESIGN SIZE: 37.1 × 29 cm.
: EXPLANATION: The harmony between Faith and Reason, illustrated by Faith writing down the dictates of Reason.
:: NOTE: The proof on p. 69 of the *Vala* manuscript lacks a few lines on the balance bar and on the lower figure's neck, hair, and gown at the waist and both feet. The upper figure lacks many lines in her hair. The text panel is 6 mm. shorter at the top than in the published state. In the water color designs, p. 42, the line marked for illustration is "*Reason* the Root; fair *Faith* is but the Flow'r;"

42. P. 93.
: LINE ILLUSTRATED: *If angels tremble, 'tis at such a sight;
: MONOGRAM INSCRIPTION, lower right margin: *WB in & s*
: IMPRINT lower left: as on pl. 39.
: DESIGN SIZE: 33.9 (top of text panel to lowest engraved line) × 29.6 cm. The imprint is 11.8 cm. below the text panel.
: EXPLANATION: Angels retiring in grief and wonder from their charge of a determined infidel.
:: NOTE: The proof on p. 85 of the *Vala* manuscript lacks the imprint and has a 3 × 5.3 cm. patch on the left margin extending into the lower half of the text panel, but is otherwise the same as the published state. In the water color designs, p. 44, two consecutive lines are marked for illustration, "*Christian* is the highest Style of Man. / And is there, who the blessed Cross wipes off"

43. P. 95.
: LINE ILLUSTRATED: *The goddess bursts in thunder and in flame;
: MONOGRAM INSCRIPTION, lower right margin: *WB inv & s*
: IMPRINT: none.
: DESIGN SIZE: 38.3 × 30.2 cm.
: EXPLANATION: A personification of Truth, as she is represented by the poet, bursting on the last moments of the sinner "in thunder and in flame."
:: NOTE: The proof on p. 109 of the *Vala* manuscript lacks some lines in the figure's hair, shading on her face, crosshatching on her left knee and right calf, and flicks on the rock beneath her left foot. In the water colors, p. 47, the same line quoted above is marked for illustration.

COPIES EXAMINED: Bancroft Library, University of California, Berkeley, California (lacks printed front-matter); Doheny Library, St. John's Seminary, Camarillo, California (uncut); GEB; HEH (two, one colored and one uncut); I; Los Angeles County Museum of Art, Los Angeles, California; N; P (three, one colored); R (two, both colored); RNE (two, one uncut); UCLA (uncut); University of California, San Diego, La Jolla, California; University of Southern California, Los Angeles, California; W. We have examined color transparencies to determine the line marked for illustration in the water color designs. The reproductions in Bentley's edition of *Vala or the Four Zoas* were examined to determine the differences between the *Vala* proofs and the published state. The proofs in the collection of Mr. Philip Hofer were not available for our inspection.

COPY REPRODUCED: RNE copy with the pages mounted on larger sheets. As with all other copies examined, several pls. (in this copy 6, 7, 8, 16, 18, 20, 27, and 32) are trimmed at the bottom, cutting off all or part of the monograms and imprints. All other copies examined are too tightly bound to permit photographing without removing the binding.

Russell #17; Keynes #70; Binyon #40-82; Bentley & Nurmi #422.

V. William Hayley: LITTLE TOM THE SAILOR, 1800.

PLATES

Four pls. printed together on one sheet, 56 × 19 cm., to form a broadside with printed area of 47.4 × 16.1 cm. Pls. 1 and 3 below have text only, but the lettering was no doubt designed by Blake as an integral part of his composition. Although only signed "*W Blake Inv*" on the third plate, Blake unquestionably designed and executed the entire broadside. See the letter to Hayley of 26 November 1800 in *The Letters of William Blake*, ed. Geoffrey Keynes (London, 1968), p. 49, in which Blake writes of his own printing of *Little Tom*.

1. Headpiece to the ballad, woodcut on pewter.
   DESIGN SIZE: 11.1 × 16.1 cm.
   NOTE: The method of woodcutting (i.e., relief engraving) on pewter is described by Blake in a memorandum on p. 10 of his *Notebook (Rossetti Manuscript)*.

2. Text plate, relief etching.
   SIZE OF TEXT AREA: 21.9 × 10 cm.
   PLATE-MARK: 22.5 × 10.8 cm.

3. Tailpiece to the ballad, woodcut on pewter (see note to pl. 1 above).
   INSCRIPTION lower right within the design: *W Blake Inv*
   DESIGN SIZE: 11.2 × 16 cm.

4. Bottom plate, with imprint only, relief etching.
   IMPRINT: *Printed for & Sold by the Widow Spicer of Folkstone | for the Benefit of her Orphans | October 5, 1800*
   SIZE OF TEXT AREA: 1.2 × 10.9 cm.
   PLATE-MARK: 3.9 × 11.9 cm.
   NOTE: The plate-mark dimensions for pls. 2 and 4 have been noted, because it is unusual to find plate-marks in impressions from plates etched in relief. No plate-mark exists for pls. 1 and 3 in the copies examined. It is very likely that these designs covered the entire surface of the plate, as is usually the case in relief engraving or etching.
   The headpiece and tailpiece of a BM Department of Prints and Drawings color tinted copy are reproduced in Binyon, pl. 61. The preliminary sketch of the headpiece now in the Victoria and Albert Museum is described and reproduced in Geoffrey Keynes ed., *Pencil Drawings by William Blake* (London, 1927), pl. 25. For details on paper, a census of copies, and a description of the very convincing Emery Walker facsimile (often mistakenly attributed to William Muir), see Geoffrey Keynes, "Blake's *Little Tom the Sailor*," *The Book Collector*, 17 (1968), 421-27, reprinted in Keynes, *Blake Studies*, 2nd ed. (Oxford, 1971), pp. 105-10.

COPIES EXAMINED: Collection of Joseph Holland, Los Angeles, California (from the W. E. Moss collection, printed in black); P (from the George C. Smith collection, printed in black and mounted and cut in the middle as reproduced here); RNE (Emery Walker facsimile).

COPY REPRODUCED: P.

Russell #18; Keynes #71; Binyon #347-348; Bentley & Nurmi #379A (379B-D are facsimiles).

VI. William Hayley: DESIGNS TO A SERIES OF BALLADS, 1802.

TITLE-PAGE:

DESIGNS | TO | *A SERIES of BALLADS,* | WRITTEN | By WILLIAM HAYLEY, Esq. | And founded on | ANECDOTES RELATING TO ANIMALS, | *Drawn, Engraved, and Published,* | BY | WILLIAM BLAKE. | With the Ballads annexed, by the Author's Permission. | [rule] | 𝕮𝖍𝖎𝖈𝖍𝖊𝖘𝖙𝖊𝖗: | Printed by J. SEAGRAVE, and sold by him and P. HUMPHRY; and by R. H. EVANS, | Pall-Mall, London, for W. BLAKE, Felpham. | 1802.

> NOTE: The *Ballads* were issued separately in the summer of 1802, one per month June through September. Each *Ballad* was bound in blue paper wrappers bearing the following titles:
>
> *Ballad the First*: A SERIES OF BALLADS. | [double rule] | 𝕹𝖚𝖒𝖇𝖊𝖗 1. | [double rule] | *The ELEPHANT.* | [double rule] | BALLAD THE FIRST.
>
> *Ballad the Second*: A SERIES OF BALLADS. | [double rule] | 𝕹𝖚𝖒𝖇𝖊𝖗 2. | [double rule] | *The EAGLE.* | [double rule] | BALLAD THE SECOND. | [double rule] | CHICHESTER: Printed by J. Seagrave, and sold by him and P. Humphry; and by R. H. Evans, | Pall-Mall, London, for W. Blake, Felpham. 1802.
>
> *Ballad the Third*: A SERIES OF BALLADS. | [double rule] | 𝕹𝖚𝖒𝖇𝖊𝖗 3. | [double rule] | *The LION.* | [double rule] | BALLAD THE THIRD. | [double rule] | CHICHESTER: Printed by J. Seagrave, and sold by him and P. Humphry; and by R. H. Evans, | Pall-Mall, London, for W. Blake, Felpham. 1802.
>
> *Ballad the Fourth*: A SERIES OF BALLADS. | [double rule] | 𝕹𝖚𝖒𝖇𝖊𝖗 4. | [double rule] | *The DOG.* | [double rule] | BALLAD THE FOURTH. | [double rule] | CHICHESTER: Printed by J. Seagrave, and sold by him and P. Humphry; and by R. H. Evans, | Pall-Mall, London, for W. Blake, Felpham. 1802.

COLLATION: 4°: *Prefatory Material and Ballad the First*: π1 A³ χ1 B⁴ χ2. *Ballad the Second*: 2π1 D-E⁴. *Ballad the Third*: 3π1 F⁴ G³. *Ballad the Fourth*: 4π1 H⁴ I² 2χ1: 35 leaves including 6 full page plates. 29.4 × 23.5 cm.

> NOTE: A1 is unsigned. In all gatherings the second leaf is signed. There is no C gathering.

PAGINATION: *Prefatory Material and Ballad the First*: π1 [A1] [i] ii-iv χ1 [1] 2-9 [10]. *Ballad the Second*: 2π1 [11] 12-26. *Ballad the Third*: 3π1 [27] 28-39 [40]. *Ballad the Fourth*: 4π1 [41] 42-45 2χ1.

CONTENTS: *Prefatory Material and Ballad the First*: π1 recto *blank*; verso, frontispiece of Adam and the beasts. [1] title-page, verso *blank*. p. [i] Preface. [χ1] recto *blank;* verso, engraving of elephant lifting man, frontispiece. p. [1] The Elephant. Ballad the First. p. [10] *blank. Ballad the Second*: 2π1 recto, engraving of mother about to rescue her child; verso *blank* p. [11] The Eagle. Ballad the Second. *Ballad the Third*: 3π1 recto, engraving of the shooting of the lion; verso *blank*. p. [27] The Lion. Ballad the Third. p. [40] *blank. Ballad the Fourth*: 4π1 recto, engraving of the dog leaping into the crocodile's jaws; verso *blank*. p. 41 The Dog. Ballad the Fourth. 2χ1 engraving of girl and statue of dog; verso *blank*.

NOTE: The 1802 *Ballads* is the product of Blake's involvement with William Hayley and should be studied in the context of the Felpham period. This biographical context has been extensively treated in "William Blake as a Private Publisher," *BNYPL*, 41 (1957), 539-60 by G. E. Bentley, Jr. N. J. Barker considered the volume in some depth bibliographically in "Some Notes on the Bibiliography of William Hayley: Part III," *Transactions of The Cambridge Bibliographical Society*, 3 (1960), 341-47, but he, in writing his article, had not examined the four complete American copies which form the basis of our discussion.

This book is more complex than would be regularly expected, for it is the product of Blake's domestic press working in conjunction with a provincial printer, J. Seagrave. Its complexity is further deepened by the disjunct state of all leaves bearing engraved illustrations. The Rosenwald copy, which is in original blue paper wrappers as issued, shows clearly that all the leaves except B2 & B3, D2 & D3, E2 & E3, F2 & F3, G1 & G2, H2 & H3, and I1 & I2 are disjunct. This confirms Barker's speculation that Blake printed his engravings only on separate quarter sheets. Whether this was due to a necessity created by a small press or simply due to preference is impossible to distinguish.

This habit of printing the engravings on quarter sheets, however, effectively destroys the reliability of watermarks as an index of printing format. It indicates though that Blake received from Seagrave the printed quires and then cut them apart before imposing the plates on the proper pages. This habit also suggests that Blake may have ordered Seagrave to leave blank leaves within the gatherings for him to remove and utilize as full page engravings at another point in the *Ballad*. It as easily suggests that Blake and Seagrave were not above manipulating the signatures so that they would reflect the final state of the book rather than the printing formula. This would seem to be confirmed by the unusual conjugacy of the first and second leaves in the G and I quires. In a quarto fold the first leaf should be conjugate with the fourth, and the second with the third leaf. In the G quire, thus, the printer has apparently signed the second leaf as though it were G1, allowing a blank quarter sheet, which was in actuality G1, to be excised and used as the frontispiece to *Ballad the Third*. Similarly, the signature in the I quire has been manipulated. That leaf which is signed as I1 was most likely in reality I2 allowing the outer fold, I1 and I4, to be removed for the imposition of the initial and terminal full page engravings of *Ballad the Fourth*. Thus, the printer's formula for *Ballad the Third* should have been $3\pi1$ F^4 G^3 ($-$G1 $= 3\pi1$), and the formula for *Ballad the Fourth* should be $4\pi1$ H^4 I^2 ($-$I1 $= 4\pi1$, $-$ I4 $= 2\chi1$) $2\chi1$.

Several problems remain however. Where does the printed leaf numbered as page 9 originate? What happened to the C gathering, and where did the remaining three full page frontispieces, $\pi1$, $\chi1$ & $2\pi1$, originate?

Keynes, p. 204, suggests that page 9, or leaf $\chi2$, was unsigned C1. However, this seems a very clumsy and expensive way to have printed the page. It was more likely printed as A4. The A gathering is the only gathering composed completely of disjunct leaves: unsigned A1 the title-page, A2 the Preface pp. [1]-2, A3 pp. 3-4. The Preface is set in an italic type and ends on the verso of the third leaf. Further, Seagrave would have required only 8 full pages of type to set these first 9 pages of *Ballad the First*. The space taken up by the headpiece and tailpiece account together for nearly one full page, so that the 9 pages could be easily filled by 8 pages of type and 2 half page engravings. Seagrave, knowing Blake would have to excise the leaf, $\chi2$, to impose the plate upon it anyway, could have easily printed it as A4 and saved himself the press run of a C gathering containing only one half page of type and 7 blank pages. Blake easily could have printed the remaining 3 frontispieces, yet unaccounted for by the printing formula, upon quarter sheets taken from a blank sheet.

The C quire is thus still missing in this explanation. Perhaps it is the result of a careless compositor confused by the publication of the book in monthly parts. On the other hand, it must be remembered that, if χ2 had been C1, it would not have borne a signature, since there was to be an engraved tailpiece positioned where a signature would have appeared. There is, consequently, no conclusive bibliographic evidence to explain the disappearance of the C gathering. We would do well, however, to recall the letter Hayley wrote to J. Johnson, transcribed in part by Barker (p. 347), which suggests that Seagrave's printing house might have been prone to errors such as this. Hayley writes that "My good Seagrave is very alert in himself, but his pressmen sometimes get drunk and vex him sorely." One of Seagrave's compositors may have simply forgotten where he left off when beginning to set the second *Ballad* in preparation for the second installment. That is, however, an admittedly thin explanation.

PLATES

Fourteen intaglio copper-plate engravings, twelve of which were designed and engraved by Blake. Two plates engraved by Blake, to be reproduced in Volume III of this publication, are not from Blake's own original designs.

1. Frontispiece, facing the general title-page. In the Rosenwald copy in parts, the pl. faces p. [i], "PREFACE."
   INSCRIPTION on base below design:

   Their strength, or speed, or vigilance, were giv'n
   In aid of our defects. In some are found
   Such teachable and apprehensive parts,
   That man's attainments in his own concerns
   Match'd with th' expertness of the brutes in theirs
   Are oft time vanquish'd and thrown far behind.
          Cowpers Task
          Book VI.

   INSCRIPTION below base, right: *Blake d & s*
   IMPRINT below base: *Publishd June 1. 1802 by W Blake Felpham*
   DESIGN SIZE, including base: 15.9 × 13.1 cm. The imprint is .7 cm. below the base of the design.
   NOTE: A proof "before the addition of the engraved signature" is listed in *Bibliotheca Bibliographici*, A Catalogue of the Library Formed by Geoffrey Keynes (London, 1964), item 594.

2. P. iv, lower third of the page with text ending "INHABITANTS OF CHICHESTER."
   INSCRIPTION below design, right: *W'B d & s*
   IMPRINT below design: *Publishd June 11 1802 by W Blake Felpham*
   DESIGN SIZE: 4.2 × 12.6 cm. The imprint is .4 cm. below the design.

3. Frontispiece to the first ballad, facing p. [1], the title-page to "THE | ELEPHANT. | *BALLAD THE FIRST.*"
   INSCRIPTION below design, right: *Blake d & sc.*
   IMPRINT below design: *Publish'd June 1. 1802 by W Blake Felpham*
   DESIGN SIZE: 14.2 × 9.8 cm. The imprint is .6 cm. below the design.

NOTE: In all copies examined, the "*c*" in "*sc.*" is defective and looks like an "*r.*"

4. P. [1], upper half of the page with text beginning "THE | ELEPHANT. | *BALLAD THE FIRST.*"
   INSCRIPTION below design, right: *Blake d & s*
   IMPRINT below design: *Publish'd June 1. 1802 by W Blake Felpham*
   OVAL DESIGN SIZE: 7.4 × 11 cm. The imprint is .2 cm. below the design.
   NOTE: Preliminary sketches appear on pages 6 and 92 upper right of Blake's *Notebook (Rossetti Manuscript)*.

5. Frontispiece to the second ballad, facing blank p. [10], with the blank verso of the engraving facing p. [11], the title-page to "THE | EAGLE. | *BALLAD THE SECOND.*" In the Rosenwald copy in parts, the pl. faces the blank verso of the blue paper cover.
   INSCRIPTION below design, right: *Blake d & s*
   IMPRINT below design: *Publishd July 1. 1802 by W Blake | Felpham*
   DESIGN SIZE: 14.4 × 10 cm. The second line of the imprint is .8 cm. below the design.
   NOTE: Blake later used this same design, reduced and with some other modifications, for pl. 2 of Hayley's *Ballads,* 1805. A sepia drawing of "The Eagle," now in the collection of Mrs. Landon K. Thorne, is described and reproduced in *The Blake Collection of W. Graham Robertson,* ed. Kerrison Preston (London, 1952), pp. 178-79 and pl. 57, and in G. E. Bentley, Jr., *The Blake Collection of Mrs. Landon K. Thorne* (New York, 1971), p. 51 and pl. XXVI. There are 2 sketches of the design in the BM Department of Prints and Drawings, both giving more prominence to the mother. A third sketch in the Rosenwald Collection is reproduced in the *Blake Newsletter,* 5 (Summer and Fall, 1971), 73.

6. P. [11], upper third of the page with text beginning "THE | EAGLE. | *BALLAD THE SECOND.*"
   INSCRIPTION below design, right: *Blake in & s.*
   IMPRINT below design: *Publish'd July 1 1802 by W Blake Felpham*
   DESIGN SIZE: 7.6 × 9.9 cm. The imprint is .2 cm. below the design.

7. P. 26, lower third of the page with text ending "*End of the Second Ballad.*"
   INSCRIPTION below design, right: *Blake in*
   IMPRINT below design: *Publish'd July 1 1802 by W Blake Felpham*
   DESIGN SIZE: 6.8 × 10.2 cm. The imprint is .2 cm. below the design.

8. Frontispiece to the third ballad, facing p. 26 with the blank verso of the engraving facing p. [27], the title-page to "THE | LION. | *BALLAD THE THIRD.*" In the Rosenwald copy in parts, the pl. faces the blank verso of the blue paper cover.
   INSCRIPTION below design, right: *Blake in & s*
   IMPRINT below design: *Publish'd Augst 5 1802 by W Blake: Felpham*
   DESIGN SIZE: 15.5 × 12.7 cm. The imprint is .3 cm. below the design.
   NOTE: Blake later used this same design, reduced and with some other modifications, for pl. 3 of Hayley's *Ballads,* 1805. A sketch of this design was sold at Sotheby's on April 29, 1862, lot 181 (to Lord Houghton, with four other items for 9 shillings). The present location of this sketch has not been traced.

9. P. [27], upper half of the page with text beginning "THE | LION. | *BALLAD THE THIRD.*"
   INSCRIPTION below design, right: *Blake inv & sc*
   IMPRINT below design: *Publish'd Augst 5: 1802. by W Blake Felpham*
   OVAL DESIGN SIZE: 7.2 × 9.5 cm. The imprint is .3 cm. below the design.

10. Frontispiece to the fourth ballad, facing blank p. [40], with the blank verso of the engraving facing p. [41], the title-page to "THE | DOG. | *BALLAD THE FOURTH.*" In the Rosenwald copy in parts, the pl. faces the blank verso of the blue paper cover.
    INSCRIPTION below design, right: *Blake inv & sc*
    IMPRINT below design: *Publish'd Septr 9: 1802 by W Blake Felpham*
    DESIGN SIZE, including border: 15.1 × 11.9 cm. The imprint is .4 cm. below the border.
    NOTE: Blake later used this same design, reduced without the border and with other modifications, for pl. 1 of Hayley's *Ballads*, 1805.

11. P. [41], upper half of the page with text beginning "THE | DOG. | *BALLAD THE FOURTH.*"
    INSCRIPTION below design, right: *Blake inv s*
    IMPRINT below design: *Publish'd Septr 9: 1802 by W Blake Felpham*
    DESIGN SIZE, including border: 9.6 × 6.6 cm. The imprint is .5 cm. below the design.

12. Facing p. 52.
    INSCRIPTION below design, right: *Blake. in: s*
    IMPRINT below design: *Publish'd Septr 9: 1802 by W Blake Felpham*
    DESIGN SIZE, including border: 13.1 × 9.4 cm. The imprint is .5 cm. below the border.
    NOTE: A proof, lacking the inscription and imprint, is described and reproduced in G. E. Bentley, Jr., "A New Blake Document: The 'Riddle' Manuscript," *The Library*, XXIV (1969), 338-43 and pl. I.

COPIES EXAMINED: GEB (front matter and first and second ballads only); HEH (2); P; R (in original parts, lacking the general title-page); RNE (front matter and first ballad only).
COPIES REPRODUCED: P (pls. 1-6, 9-12); HEH (pls. 7-8).
Russell #19; Keynes #72; Binyon #83-94; Bentley & Nurmi #375.

VII. William Hayley:
THE LIFE AND POSTHUMOUS WRITINGS OF WILLIAM COWPER, 1803 & 1804.

TITLE-PAGE, Volume I, first edition:
THE | LIFE, | AND | *POSTHUMOUS WRITINGS*, | OF | WILLIAM COWPER, Esqr. | WITH AN | INTRODUCTORY LETTER | TO THE | *RIGHT HONOURABLE EARL COWPER.* | [double rule] | By WILLIAM HAYLEY, Esqr. | [double rule] | "Obversatur oculis ille vir, quo neminem ætas nostra graviorem, sanctiorem, subtiliorem | "denique tulit: quem ego quum ex admiratione diligere cœpissem, quod evenire contra solet, | "magis admiratus sum, postquam penitus inspexi. Inspexi enim penitus: nihil a me ille secretum, | "non joculare, non serium, non triste, non lætum." | [to the right] Plinii Epist. Lib. 4, Ep. 17. | [rule] | VOL. I. | [double rule] | 𝕮𝖍𝖎𝖈𝖍𝖊𝖘𝖙𝖊𝖗: | *Printed by J. Seagrave;* | FOR J. JOHNSON, ST. PAUL'S CHURCH-YARD, LONDON. | [rule] | 1803.

COLLATION: 4°: π^2 a-b^{2}c^1 A-B^2 B-3F^4 3G^3: 218 leaves + 2 plates. 27 × 21.5 cm.

PAGINATION: [2 pp.] [I-III] IV-XII [8 pp.] [1] 2-144 [115] 116-413 [414].

CONTENTS: [2 pp.] half title-page, verso *blank*. p. [I] title-page, verso *blank*. p. [III] An Introductory Letter to the Right Honourable Earl Cowper. [8 pp.] Contents. p. [1] The Life of Cowper, Part the First. p. [115] Part the Second. p. [414] *blank*.

> NOTE: The Contents quire was originally published at the end of the volume, as demonstrated by the uncut copy in original boards at UCLA. Binders have usually moved it forward to the position here described. Norma Russell, in her description of this project, *A Bibliography of William Cowper to 1837* (Oxford, 1963), pp. 250-53, places the quire at the beginning of the book before the Introductory Letter.

TITLE-PAGE, Volume II, first edition: Identical to Volume I except for volume number.

COLLATION: 4°: π^2 a^4 B-3F^4 3G^4 (3G + χ1) 3H^2: 217 leaves + 1 plate.

PAGINATION: [12 pp.] [1] 2-290 [291] 292-303 [304] 305-321 [322] 323-344 [345] 346-380 [381] 382-385 [386] 387-388 [389] 390-393 [394] 395-415 [416-417] 418-422.

CONTENTS: [2. pp.] half title-page, verso *blank*. [2 pp.] title-page, verso *blank*. [6 pp.] Contents. [2 pp.] *blank*. [1] The Life of Cowper, Part the Third. p. [291] Appendix. (No. 1.) Original Poems. p. [304] Appendix. (No. 2.) Translations of Greek Verses. p. [322] Appendix. (No. 3) Translations from Horace and Virgil. p. [345] Appendix. (No. 4.) Translations from various Latin Poems of Vincent Bourne, and a few Epigrams of Owen. p. [381] Appendix (No. 5.) Montes Glaciales [and] On the Ice Islands. p. [386] Appendix. (No. 6.) Verses to the Memory of Dr. Lloyd. p. [389]

Appendix. (No. 7.) Translations from the Fables of Gay. p. [394] Appendix. (No. 8.) The Connoisseur. (Nos. 119, 134, 138). p. 415 Appendix. Motto on a Clock [and engraving]. p. [416] Conclusion. p. [417] The Conclusion.

TITLE-PAGE, Volume III, first edition: Like Volumes I & II, except for the following variations. The word "LETTER" is followed by a comma. In the inscription the word "*neminem*" is changed to "*neminen*," and a period replaces the comma after "4." Then: | [rule] | VOL. III. | [double rule] | 𝕮𝖍𝖎𝖈𝖍𝖊𝖘𝖙𝖊𝖗: | *PRINTED BY J. SEAGRAVE;* | FOR J. JOHNSON, ST. PAUL'S CHURCH-YARD, LONDON. | [rule] | 1804.

COLLATION: 4°: π² *² A-D⁴ A-3E⁴ 3F² 3G⁴ (−3G3= *1, −3G4= *2) : 228 leaves + 2 plates.
> NOTE: The Princeton copy in original boards, uncut, shows the * quire to be part of the 3G quire.

PAGINATION: [8 pp.] [i-ii] iii-xxxi [xxxii] [1] 2-402 [403-405] 406-408 [409] 410-416.

CONTENTS: [2 pp.] half title-page, verso *blank*. [2 pp.] title-page, verso *blank*. [4 pp.] Contents. p. [i] fly title-page, verso *blank*. p. [iii] Desultory Remarks. &c. p. [xxxii] *blank*. p. [1] The Life of Cowper, Part the Fourth. p. 373 Twelve Letters, Written in the Early Part of the Poet's Life, to His Relation, The Lady Hesketh. p. [403] [A Dedication] to William Aiton. p. [404] *blank*. p. [405] Preface to the Poem on Yardley-Oak. p. [409] Yardley-Oak.
> NOTE: p. 416 has the following imprint: [double rule] | SEAGRAVE, PRINTER, | 𝕮𝖍𝖎𝖈𝖍𝖊𝖘𝖙𝖊𝖗.

TITLE-PAGE, Volume I, second edition: Like Volume III to: | VOL. I | [rule] | SECOND EDITION. | [double rule] | 𝕮𝖍𝖎𝖈𝖍𝖊𝖘𝖙𝖊𝖗: | *PRINTED BY J. SEAGRAVE;* | FOR J. JOHNSON, ST. PAUL'S CHURCH-YARD, LONDON. | [rule] | 1803.

COLLATION: With the exception of the missing half title-page the collation is identical to that of Volume I, first edition. The text is completely re-set, however, and this creates some deviation which will identify it. Generally, there are fewer ligatures in the re-set text, and capitalization varies. For example, on p. III, third line, the word "subject" lacks the ct ligature in the second edition. Further, p. 1 has been lengthened by one line, changing the catch-word from "hold" to "Inn." In the second edition, the lines of spaced periods, utilized as rules throughout the text in the first edition, are replaced by double lines. Also, in the second edition of Volume I, p. 179 is incorrectly numbered 176. PAGINATION and CONTENTS are identical to those in the first edition.

TITLE-PAGE, Volume II, second edition: Same as Volume I except for volume number.

COLLATION: 4°: a⁴ (−a1 = title-page, −a2 signed a, −a4 = b1) B-3G⁴ χ 3H³: 216 leaves + 2 plates.

PAGINATION and CONTENTS: The first edition is followed closely, but the contents section has been re-set in smaller type reducing the number of pages by 2. From pp. 1-380 pagination is identical. However, a new poem, "The Cantab.," has been added to

p. 377 making it necessary to displace the text following by one page. Thus, Appendix. (No. 5.) now begins on p. 382 and so on. The inserted leaf bearing Blake's design, reproduced in this volume, was in the first edition on p. 415 but is reworked and renumbered in the second edition. (See plate descriptions below).

NOTE: There is no second edition of Volume III.

According to Barker in "Some Notes on the Bibliography of William Hayley: Part III," p. 347, Volume I of Hayley's *Life of Cowper* was printed by September of 1802, and Volume II was ready by December of the same year. The two volumes were published early in 1803 and enjoyed an immediate success. Volume III was published early in 1804 with the second edition of Volumes I & II, which explains why the title-pages of the second edition should exhibit the same variations as Volume III.

Large paper copies of the first edition (HEH) display some interesting indices of their early printing. It is likely that these uncommon copies were pre-publication copies perhaps like those Norma Russell records as being sent to Lady Hesketh (p. 252, n. 4). Volume III of the HEH large paper copy displays these most easily identifiable indices: 1) a variant state of the fly-title to Desultory Remarks which reads: DESULTORY REMARKS | ON THE | *LETTERS of EMINENT PERSONS,* | PARTICULARLY THOSE OF | POPE AND COWPER. | [rule] | "EPISTOLÆ VITAM IPSAM HOMINIS REPRÆSENTANT."——— ERASMUS. | [double rule]. The regular issue of this volume contains the regular fly-title which is identical except the Latin inscription is in lower-case, the fifth line reads "POPE and COWPER" and is followed not by a single rule but by a double rule. 2) on p. 17 the HEH copy displays in the volume number that accompanies the signature this aberration: "VOL˙ III." which is corrected in later copies. 3) on p. 142 the HEH copy reads at the beginning of the letter: "MY DEAR FRIEND." The regular issue (ABF, RNE) has lost the M of "MY" during the press run, either by wear or by an an accident of printing. 3) on p. 345 the catchword "MENDS" loosens as the printing progresses. Consequently, an early state, such as the HEH large paper copy, will show the catchword properly aligned, while the later copies or regular issues will show this catchword with the "D" and "S" floating upwards and the other letters going slightly askew as the form loosens. We can thus, with these indices, remark with some confidence whether a copy is early or late from the press.

The paper encountered in this publication varies greatly, but two basic distinctions must be made. The large paper copies are printed on J. Whatman paper displaying the mark comparable to #3460 in Edward Heawood's *Watermarks Mainly of the 17th and 18th Centuries* (Hilversum, Holland, 1950). Regular issues of the books were printed on less expensive papers bearing a variety of watermarks and some bearing none at all. In most copies examined, the paper was marked only by a countermarked date, 1801, 1802, or 1803. However, there are two more elaborate watermarks which appear in most copies, though less frequently. The first appears in the position of a countermark as C 1802 or C 1803. The second is more unusual since the 1801 date appears in the position of a countermark—in the lower external margin—and two initials, EM, appear irregularly in the upper margin. The position of these initials is unusual since they lie parallel to the fold and are often separated from each other by the trimming of the fold in the binding process. The normal position of a watermark in a quarto format should be in the inner margin; however, by the early nineteenth century in printing, many papers are machine made, and the custom of watermarking papers grows very irregular.

Two exceptionally fine uncut and unopened copies of the trade edition are to be found in the Princeton and UCLA collections. The UCLA copy is interesting since it is loosely bound. Several quires may be removed and unfolded into their original form as sheets, because they were not sewn in.

For further discussion of this work see: G. E. Bentley, Jr., "Blake, Hayley, and Lady Hesketh," *Review of English Studies*, N.S. 7, No. 27 (1956), 265-86, and "William Blake and Johnny of Norfolk," *Studies in Philology*, 53, No. 1 (1956), 60-74.

PLATES

Six intaglio copper-plate engravings, all engraved by Blake, with one also designed by him.

1A. First published state appearing in the first ed., vol. II, p. 415, lower three-quarters of the page beneath title "APPENDIX. | *MOTTO on a CLOCK*," and text ending *"Waiting to seize it—vigilantly wait!"*
INSCRIPTION on the base of the weather-house:

> *Peace to the Artist whose ingenious thought*
> *Devised the Weather-house, that useful toy!*
> *Fearless of humid air and gathering rains*
> *Forth steps the Man, an emblem of myself,*
> *More delicate his tim'rous mate retires.*   *Task. B 1. line 200*

INSCRIPTION below left side of the base of the weather-house: *Blake d & sc*
INSCRIPTION on the banner above the hares: THE PEASANTS NEST
INSCRIPTION beneath the hares: PUSS TINEY & BESS
INSCRIPTION lower left and right of the hares: *Cowper's* [design] *tame Hare's*
IMPRINT below design, printed too lightly to read in many copies: *Publish'd Novr 5 1802 by J Johnson St Pauls Church Yard*
DESIGN SIZE: 15.2 × 11.6 cm. The imprint is .7 cm. below the design.
> NOTE: Printed on the verso, p. [416], are four lines of Latin verse with Cowper's five line translation beneath.

1B. Second published state appearing in at least one copy of the first ed. (see note below) and in the second ed., vol. II, p. [415], lower three-quarters of the page beneath title "MOTTO ON A CLOCK." and text ending as in first state.
INSCRIPTION, IMPRINT, DESIGN SIZE, AND TEXT on verso: as in first state.
> NOTE: The engraving has been considerably reworked in the second state, with many lines strengthened and darkened. Small dots have been added to the sun left of the girl and another line engraved beneath her feet. Lines have been added to the sky behind the man, to the trunks of the 3 trees, and to the garland, particularly just above and below the inscribed banner. A small waving line now appears just before the base of the "*P*" in "*Peace*" in the first inscription quoted above. The ground beneath the hares and the trees to their right have been darkened. The general strengthening of the engraving, and perhaps more care in printing, has resulted in a much better impression in most copies of the second ed. than in the first. This second state is reproduced in Thomas Wright, *The Life of William Blake* (Olney, 1929), I, pl. 38 and in Ruthven Todd, *William Blake the Artist* (London and New York, 1971), p. 61.
>
> In one Princeton copy of the first ed. (Ex 3693.7.716.1803cq) the second state of the engraving appears on p. [415]. The plate was apparently re-worked before at least one copy of the first ed. had been printed, very likely in response to the poor impressions produced from the plate in the first state. Keynes (p.

39

251) writes that he has "noticed at least three states" of this engraving. This third state in the Keynes collection appears to be intermediate between the two listed here, showing (Keynes tells us) the added work on the ground beneath the hares but without the other additional work noted above. The Keynes print is on a loose sheet with the typographic setting of the first ed. and an 1802 watermark. We have found no copy of *The Life of Cowper* with the engraving in this state. It may be a proof pulled in the course of reworking the plate while the last copies of the first ed. were being printed.

We wish to thank Sir Geoffrey Keynes for information on the print in his collection.

COPIES EXAMINED: ABF (first ed.); GEB (2 copies of first ed., one of second ed.); HEH (first and second ed.); N (first ed.); P (4 copies of first ed., including one uncut in original boards and one with the second state of the engraving, and one of the second ed.); R (loose pl. in first state); RNE (first and second ed., loose pl. of first state); UCLA (first ed. uncut in original boards); UW (first ed.); W (first ed. and loose pl. of first state).

COPY REPRODUCED: ABF.

Russell #96 ; Keynes #124; Binyon, not listed; Bentley & Nurmi #377.

VIII. William Hayley: BALLADS, 1805.

TITLE-PAGE:

BALLADS, | BY | *WILLIAM HAYLEY, Esq.* | FOUNDED ON | ANECDOTES RE-LATING TO ANIMALS, | WITH | *PRINTS,* | DESIGNED AND ENGRAVED | By WILLIAM BLAKE. | [double rule] | Chichester: Printed by J. Seagrave; | FOR RICHARD PHILLIPS, BRIDGE-STREET, | BLACKFRIARS, LONDON. | [rule] | 1805.

> NOTE: One variant has been noted in a Princeton copy (Ex 3776.3.314 c.2), the Newberry copy, and in the Doheny copy: in these copies a comma appears after BLAKE, rather than the period here described.

COLLATION: $8°$: π^3 A-N^8 O^3 : 110 leaves + 5 plates. 17.1 cm. × 10.7 cm.

> NOTE: Keynes (p. 207) and Barker in "Some Notes on the Bibliography of William Hayley," p. 341, describe the first and last quires as quarto. It is clear, however, from the uncut RNE copy in original boards that this is not the case. The blank leaf which Keynes and Barker add at π^1 and O4 is in fact a free end paper removed from the original boards. That this free end paper is made from the same stock as the text paper confuses the issue. It is likely that π^3 was printed as part of the O gathering and repositioned during binding.

PAGINATION: [6pp.] [1] 2-12 [13] 14-21 [22] 23-37 [38] 39-50 [51] 52-60 [61] 62-69 [70] 71-84 [85] 86-99 [100] 101-112 [113] 114-122 [123] 124-136 [137] 138-149 [150] 151-160 [161] 162-183 [184] 185-203 [204] 205-212 [213-214].

CONTENTS: 2pp. half-title page, verso *blank*. 2 pp. title-page, verso *blank*. 2pp. Preface, verso *blank*. p. [1] The Dog, Ballad the First. p. [13] The Elephant, Ballad the Second. p. [22] The Eagle, Ballad the Third. p. [38] The Stag, Ballad the Fourth. p. [51] The Stork, Ballad the Fifth. p. [61] The Panther, Ballad the Sixth. p. [70] The Grateful Snake, Ballad the Seventh. p. [85] The Fatal Horse, Ballad the Eighth. p. [100] The Lion, Ballad the Ninth. p. [113] The Swan, Ballad the Tenth. p. [123] The Hermit's Dog, Ballad the Eleventh. p. [137] The Halcyon, Ballad the Twelfth. p. [150] The Serpents, Ballad the Thirteenth. p. [161] The Goat, Ballad the Fourteenth. p. [184] The Baya: or The Indian Bird, Ballad the Fifteenth. p. [204] The Horse, Ballad the Sixteenth. p. [213] Index. p. [214] *blank*.

> NOTE: Imprint on p. [213]: [rule] | CHICHESTER: PRINTED BY J. SEAGRAVE. Ballad the Fifteenth, The Baya, is printed in smaller type to allow for the longer lines to be printed without breaking.

PLATES

Five intaglio copper-plate engravings, all designed and engraved by Blake. A set of "proofs before letters" was sold at the MacGeorge sale at Sotheby's on July 1, 1924 (lot 122). These are probably the proofs signed "Blake inv. & sc." but without the inscriptions listed in *William Blake: The Description of a Small Collection of His Works in the Library of a New York Collector* (New York, 1927), p. 12. This "collector" was in fact George C. Smith, who sold the proofs with the rest of his collection at Parke-Bernet on Nov. 2, 1938 (lot 51). Their present location is not known. A copy of the book in the collection of S. Foster Damon has hand-colored plates, possibly by Blake himself.

1A. Frontispiece, first published state facing the title-page.
   INSCRIPTION below design: *Blake. inv & s | The Dog,*
   IMPRINT below inscription: *Pub.^{d} June, 18, 1805, by R Phillips N 6, Bridge Street. Black Friers.*
   DESIGN SIZE: 11.3 × 7.1 cm. The imprint is 1.6 cm. below the design.
   NOTE: Blake had previously used a larger version of this design, with a border and several other differences, for pl. 10 of *Designs to a Series of Ballads,* 1802.

1B. Frontispiece, second published state facing p. [1] in the Princeton, Newberry, and Doheny copies with variant title-page and facing the title-page in the GEB and UW copies with standard title-page.
   INSCRIPTIONS, IMPRINT, AND DESIGN SIZE: as in first state.
   NOTE: In the second state, the crosshatching in the upper left corner has been deepened and new lines have been added to the cliff just below the man. This second state is reproduced in Thomas Wright, *The Life of William Blake* (Olney, 1929), II, pl. 48, Morchard Bishop, *Blake's Hayley* (London, 1951), following p. 160, and Ruthven Todd, *William Blake the Artist* (London and New York, 1971), p. 66.

2A. First published state facing p. [22].
   INSCRIPTION below design: *Blake inv & s | The Eagle,*
   IMPRINT below inscription: *Pub.^{d} June, 18, 1805, by R. Phillips, N° 6 Bridge Street Black Friers.*
   DESIGN SIZE: 10.8 × 7 cm. The imprint is 1.8 cm. below the design.
   NOTE: The period at the end of the imprint is .3 cm. to the right of the last word. Blake had previously used a larger and slightly different version of this design for pl. 5 of *Designs to a Series of Ballads,* 1802.

2B. Second published state facing p. [34] in the Princeton and Newberry copies with variant title-page, facing p. [22] in the Doheny copy with variant title-page, and facing p. [22] in the GEB and UW copies with standard title-page.
   INSCRIPTIONS, IMPRINT, AND DESIGN SIZE: as in first state.
   NOTE: In the second state, the clouds on the left margin of the plate have been obscured by darkening with waving lines. The eagle's wings have been darkened, and lines have been added to the child's gown, the woman's dress, and the rocks both beneath the woman and on the lower right. This second published state is reproduced in T. S. R. Boase, *English Art 1800-1870* (Oxford, 1959), pl. 20a, Kathleen Raine, *William Blake* (London and New York, 1970), fig. 99, and G. E. Bentley, Jr., *The Blake Collection of Mrs. Landon K. Thorne* (New York, 1971), pl. XXVII.

3A. First published state facing p. [100].
   INSCRIPTION below design: *Blake inv. & s | The Lion*
   IMPRINT below inscription: *Pub'd June 18, 1805 by R Phillips N° 6 Bridge Street Black Friers.*

DESIGN SIZE: 10.9 × 7 cm. The imprint is 1.7 cm. below the design.

> NOTE: Blake had previously used a larger and slightly different version of this design for pl. 8 of *Designs to a Series of Ballads*, 1802.

3B. Second published state facing p. [100] in the Princeton, Newberry, and Doheny copies with variant title-page, and in the GEB and UW copies with standard title-page.
INSCRIPTION, IMPRINT, AND DESIGN SIZE: as in first state.

> NOTE: In the second state, the sky has been darkened with parallel horizontal lines just above the point at which the palm trunk meets the left margin of the design. Lines have been added to the sky above the lion's body and around his tail, to the river, to the back of the woman with a bow, and to the cliff below the lion. This second published state is reproduced in Bernard Blackstone, *English Blake* (Cambridge, 1949), pl. III top.

4. Facing p. [123].
INSCRIPTION below design: *Blake inv & sc | The Hermits Dog,*
IMPRINT below inscription: *Pub^d June 18, 1805, by R. Phillips N° 6 Bridge Street Black Friers*
DESIGN SIZE: 10.7 × 7.4 cm. The imprint is 1.9 cm. below the design.

> NOTE: The plate in the Doheny, GEB, Newberry, Princeton, and UW copies with the second state of pls. 1-3 appears to be of the same state as those in all other copies examined. The very slight differences in tone may be accounted for plausibly by differences in inking.

5. Facing p. [204].
INSCRIPTION below design: *Blake inv & sc. | The Horse*
IMPRINT below inscription: *Pub^d June, 18, 1805 by R. Phillips N° 6, Bridge Street Black Friers.*
DESIGN SIZE: 10.7 × 7.2 cm. The imprint is 1.9 cm. below the design.

> NOTE: The plate is bound facing p. [85] in the Princeton and Doheny copies with variant title-page. The plate in the Princeton, Doheny, GEB, Newberry, and UW copies with the second state of pls. 1-3 appears to be of the same state as those in all other copies examined. The very slight differences in tone may be accounted for plausibly by differences in inking. The tempera painting on copper of this design is described and reproduced in *Painting in England 1700-1850: Collection of Mr. & Mrs. Paul Mellon* (Richmond, Virginia, 1963), I, no. 382 and II, pl. 17. A proof in the collection of Mr. Raymond Lister, Cambridge, England lacks some shading on the horse, the shading on the woman's arms, neck, and face, and many details of the child's face. This proof, bound into an extra-illustrated first edition of Gilchrist's *Life of Blake* (1863), has the title inscription *"The Horse,"* but lacks the signature. It is trimmed too close on the lower margin to reveal any imprint, if present.
>
> We wish to thank Mr. Raymond Lister for information on the proof in his collection.

COPIES EXAMINED: Doheny Library, St. John's Seminary, Camarillo, California (with variant title-page and second state of pls. 1-3); GEB (uncut, with second state of pls. 1-3); HEH (first state); I (with the first state of all pls.); N (with variant title-page and second state of pls. 1-3); P(2, one with variant title-page and second state of pls. 1-3, the other with first state); R (three sets of loose pls., one with pls. 2-4 only, all first state); RNE (uncut in original boards with first state of all plates and loose pls. 1-4 in the first state); UW (2, one with second state of pls. 1-3, the other with first state).

COPIES REPRODUCED: HEH (pls. 1-3); P (pls. 4, 5).

Russell #20; Keynes #74; Binyon #95-99; Bentley & Nurmi #374.

IX. THE PROLOGUE AND CHARACTERS OF CHAUCER'S PILGRIMS, 1812.

TITLE-PAGE:

THE | PROLOGUE AND CHARACTERS | OF | 𝕮𝖍𝖆𝖚𝖈𝖊𝖗'𝖘 𝕻𝖎𝖑𝖌𝖗𝖎𝖒𝖘, | SELECTED FROM HIS | CANTERBURY TALES; | INTENDED TO ILLUSTRATE | A PARTICULAR DESIGN | OF | Mr. WILLIAM BLAKE, | WHICH IS ENGRAVED BY HIMSELF. | And may been at Mr. COLNAGHI's, Cockspur Street; at | Mr. BLAKE's, No. 28, Broad Street, Golden Square; and at the | Publisher's, Mr. HARRIS, Bookseller, St. Paul's Church Yard. | [rule] | *PRICE TWO SHILLINGS AND SIXPENCE.* | [rule] | M.-DCCC.XII.

> NOTE: On the verso of the title-leaf is this imprint: "[rule] | G. Smeeton, Printer, 139, St. Martin's Lane." The title-page is reproduced in Keynes, p. 210.

COLLATION: 8°: [A]² [B]⁴ C- I⁴ : 34 leaves + 1 inserted plate. 18 × 11.3 cm.

PAGINATION: [i-iii] iv [1-3] 4-61 [62].

CONTENTS: p. [i] title-page, verso *blank* except for imprint. p. [iii] Preface. p. [1] *blank*. p. [2] Chaucer. The Prologue. p. [3] Translation. Prologue to the Tales. p. [6] Chaucer. Characters of the Pilgrims. The Knight. p. [7] Translation. Characters of the Pilgrims. The Knight. p. 8 The Squire. p. 9 the Squire. p. 10 The Squire's Yeoman. p. 11 The Squire's Yeoman. | The Prioress. p. 12 The Prioresse. p. 14 The Monke. p. 15 The Monk. p. 17 The Fryar. p. 18 The Frere. p. 21 The Merchant. | The Clerk or Scholar of Oxford. p. 22 The Merchaunt. p. 24 The Clerke of Oxenford. p. 25 The Man of Law, &c. p. 26 The Sergeant at Law. p. 27 The Franklin, or Country Gentleman. p. 28 The Frankelein. p. 29 The Haberdasher; Weaver; Carpenter; Dyer, Tap'stry Merchant. p. 30 The Haberdasher. | The Coke. p. 32 The Shipman. p. 33 The Cooke. | The Shipman or Seaman, &c. p. 34 The Doctor of Phisike. p. 35 The Doctor of Physick. p. 36 The Wife of Bathe. p. 38 The Parsone. p. 39 The Wife of Bath. p. 41 The Parson. p. 42 The Plowman. p. 44 The Miller. p. 46 The Manciple. | The Reve. p. 50 The Sompnour. p. 51 The Plowman, &c. p. 52 The Pardoner. p. 53 The Miller. | The Manciple, or Temple Treasurer. p. 55 The Reve, or Steward. p. 59 The Sumner, or Apparitor. p. 60 The Pardoner. p. [62] Errata.

> NOTE: Two texts are yoked together to juxtapose Chaucer's Middle English text and a modernization. Chaucer's Middle English text is taken from the 1687 edition of Thomas Speight, enclosed in a ruled frame and printed on the even numbered pages. On the odd numbered pages is the "Translation" or modernized version taken from Ogle's 1741 edition. Speight's text is slightly shorter than Ogle's and thus ends on p. 58, leaving the translation to spend itself on pages 59-61.
>
> While the book is signed in fours it appears from the evidence of the watermarks to have been printed by half sheet imposition, and thus its format is in reality octavo. Two different watermarks appear in the quires. In the external two quires [A]² and I⁴ the watermark L TOVIL MILL | 1810 appears passing through the hinge.

45

The mark is that of the Lower Tovil Mill, Maidstone Parish, Kent. See A. H. Shorter's *Paper Mills and Papermakers in England 1495-1800* (Hilversum, Holland, 1957) pp. 190-91. The internal quires, B-H, are marked with an edge watermark, "1809." When taken together, 8 copies (2 HEH, R, Trinity College, Yale, BM, 2 Pierpont Morgan), evidence a clearly observable tendency for half the quires to be marked and half to be unmarked. See chart: X indicates no watermark in the quire.

	B	C	D	E	F	G	H
HEH [Hoe copy]	X	X	D1	E1	X	X	H1
HEH [Edelheim copy]	B1	C1	D2	X	F2	G2	H2
Rosenwald	B1	X	X	X	X	X	X
Trinity College	B1	C1	D2	E2	F1	G2	H2
Yale	B2	C2	D1	E1	F1	G1	X
British Museum	X	C2	D1	E1	F1	G2	X
Pierpont Morgan	X	X	D2	X	X	X	X
Pierpont Morgan (Thorne)	X	C2	D1	X	X	G2	H2

No gathering always shows the watermark and, in the 8 copies examined, 33 quires were marked and 23 were unmarked. The meaning of this is clearly that the volume was printed on half sheets of Post paper and gathered in half sheets. We are indebted especially to Mr. Paul Needham of the Pierpont Morgan for assisting us in the description of their copies. The Pierpont Morgan's uncut Thorne copy shows clear signs of tearing, where in a regular quarto only deckled edges should appear. This evidence conclusively establishes the octavo format of the printing. An additional index of half sheet imposition is the fact that the watermark only appears on the first and second leaves of each gathering. In a regular quarto the side watermark should appear irregularly on all leaves. But, in a book printed by imposition on halfsheets, a side watermark, or countermark, will appear only on leaves carrying printed pages, the type for which was situated at the four corners of the form. For the positioning of a form in "two half sheets worked together" see T. C. Hansard's *Typographia* (London, 1825), p. 506.

PLATES

Two intaglio copper-plate engravings, both designed and engraved by Blake. See note on pl. 2 for details on its attribution.

1. Frontispiece, facing the title-page.
    INSCRIPTION AND IMPRINT below the design:

    Reeve. Chaucer. Oxford. Cook.   *Miller. Wife of Merchant.*
        Scholar.   *Bath.*

                                                                                W Blake

    Publish'd Dec.r 26. 1811. by Newberry St Pauls Ch:Yard   *inv & sc*

    DESIGN SIZE: 11.6 × 7.2 cm. The imprint is .8 cm. below the design.

    NOTE: The design is basically the same as the left section of Blake's large separate plate of "Chaucer's Canterbury Pilgrims" with several changes in scale and details, most notably in the inscription over the portal of the Tabarde, the number and configuration of the white birds on the roof, and the Gothic architecture seen through the portal and in the background. The separate plate is described and reproduced in Geoffrey Keynes, *Engravings by William Blake: The Separate Plates* (Dublin, 1956), pp. 45-49 and pls. 27-33. A pencil sketch for the separate plate was sold by Frederick Tatham at Sotheby's, April 29, 1862 (lot 161) and later by Henry Cunliffe at Sotheby's, May 5, 1895 (lot 100). Keynes, *Engravings by Blake: The Separate Plates* (p. 49), reports that the drawing is in the collection of Lord Cunliffe. The large tempera painting of the same subject in the Stirling-Maxwell Collection of the Glasgow Museums and Art Galleries is described and reproduced in Keynes, *The Tempera Paintings of William Blake* (London, 1951), pp. 15-16 and frontispiece.

2. P. 58, lower third of the page below printed text ending "My wit is short, ye may well understand."
   INSCRIPTION: none.
   DESIGN SIZE: 3.3 × 5.9 cm.
   NOTE: Although unsigned, this plate was very probably designed and engraved by Blake. Since the book is in part intended as an advertisement for Blake's large plate of the Canterbury Pilgrims, it is most unlikely that any other artist or engraver would be commissioned to produce this single vignette.

COPIES EXAMINED: HEH (2); R; BM (examined for us by Howard M. Nixon); Peirpont Morgan (two, examined for us by Paul Needham); Trinity College (examined for us by Peter J. Knapp); Yale (examined for us by Christina M. Hanson).
COPY REPRODUCED: R.
Russell #25; Keynes #75; Binyon #101 (pl. 1 only); Bentley & Nurmi #359 (pl. 1 only).

X. Robert John Thornton: THE PASTORALS OF VIRGIL, 1821.

TITLE-PAGE, Volume I:

THE | *PASTORALS* | OF | VIRGIL, | WITH A COURSE | OF | ENGLISH READING, | ADAPTED FOR SCHOOLS: | IN WHICH ALL | THE PROPER FACILITIES | ARE GIVEN, ENABLING YOUTM [sic] TO ACQUIRE | THE LATIN LANGUAGE, | IN | *THE SHORTEST PERIOD OF TIME.* | Illustrated by 230 Engravings. | [double rule] | BY | ROBERT JOHN THORNTON, M.D. | MEMBER OF THE UNIVERSITY OF CAMBRIDGE, &c. &c. | [rule] | THIRD EDITION. | [rule] | VOL. I. | *LONDON:* | Stereotyped and Printed by J. M'Gowan, Great Windmill Street. | Published by F. C. & J. Rivingtons; Longman and Co.; Sherwood | and Co.; Whittaker and Co.; Cadell and Co.; Arch and Co.; Black | and Co.; J. Richardson; Asperne; Souter; Sir Richard Phillips and | Co.; Rodwell and Co.; Gosling; Cox; Highly; Bumpus; Sharp; | and may be had of all Booksellers in the United Kingdom; or of Mr. | Harrison, 13, Little Tower Street, Agent for Dr. Thornton. | 1821. | *N. B. The Price of Thornton's Pastorals of Virgil, is* 15*s. bound.* | A full Allowance to the Trade and Schoolmasters.

> NOTE: In all copies examined the O of "*PERIOD*" is broken at the top, and the apostrophe in "J. M'Gowan" is inverted.

COLLATION: 12°: π^6 (-π5) χ^6 a^6 (-a1 & a2) b^6 B-S^6 T^5: 128 leaves + 69 leaves bearing illustrations + 2 folding plates. 17.5 × 10.4 cm.

> NOTE: The third leaf is always signed as though it were the second leaf, following the unusual practice, described in R. W. Chapman's article, "Notes on Eighteenth-Century Bookbuilding," *Library,* 4th Ser., IV (1924), 180, of signing a 12mo in sixes with the third leaf always signed as though it were the second leaf. Thus in the "a" gathering, even though the first leaf in the gathering is signed "a2," two initial leaves are cancelled.
>
> Keynes (p. 212) describes the preliminary pages thus: *[8-1] a-b^6. However, the matter seems to be more complicated than Keynes suggests. We have, using the evidence of pagination, signatures, and content blocks, been able to be more precise in our description. We have designated the unsigned 6 leaves of the Contents table as a separate gathering, χ^6. What remains are 2 groups of leaves, the first showing a small roman numeral, vi, as its first page number, the second showing a v, indicating that apparently 4 unsigned, unnumbered pages preceded each roman numeral sequence. Only one such group of 4 unsigned and unnumbered pages exists however, the title-leaf and preface-leaf. We surmise, thus, that 2 leaves, which would have begun the second roman numeral sequence, have been cancelled. But which pair? The second roman numeral sequence begins the preface which runs through p. xxiv. The first sequence includes a 3 page Address to School Masters & Parents, a ½ page quotation from Cicero, and a 3 page listing of Opinions in Favor of the Present Plan of Teaching. These small preliminaries seem reasonably to precede the 20 page Preface. The binders of the volume thought so too, for each copy examined placed them before the Preface. Consequently, it is this second roman numeral sequence which has lost 4 pages.
>
> In the π quire, our designation for the first roman numeral sequence, another page has for some reason been cancelled. Assuming that this roman numeral sequence is

continuous, we can infer the missing page numbers forward from vi through the title-page as [i], but continuing back into the quire we find that there are only 2 leaves upon which we must place 6 page numbers. Between the leaf numbered on its verso, vi, and the last numbered leaf, xi-xii, there are only 2 leaves. Examining closely the prefatory material following the first numbered page, we discover that in the section of Opinions in Favor of the Present Plan of Teaching, the fourth opinion is missing, since the numbering of opinions skips from 3 to 5. The missing leaf then must have followed that upon which the section of Opinions began, [vii-viii], but preceded the last leaf of opinions, xi-xii. In other words, π5 or pp. ix-x has been cancelled. This fourth opinion must have been important for it required 2 complete pages, and one can only guess why it became necessary to eliminate it.

Since this 1821 edition is a stereotyped edition, presumably the earlier editions will display the pages here cancelled. However, after an extensive search, we have not been able to trace the earlier editions. Apparently, since they lack the valuable Blake connection, they have not been widely collected, rendering them considerably more rare than the 1821 edition.

The 6 leaves upon which Blake's wood engravings are printed are placed among the c gathering thus: *1 [i, Frontispiece on verso, recto *blank*], C1, *2 [ii-v on recto, verso *blank*], *3 [vi-ix on verso, recto *blank*], C2, *4 [x-xiii on recto, verso *blank*], *5 [xiv-xvi on verso, recto *blank*], C3 [signed C2], *6 [xvii-xx on recto, verso *blank*] C4, C5, C6.

PAGINATION: [i-v] vi [vii-viii] (ix-x *missing*) xi-xii [1] 2-12 (i-iv *missing*) v-xxiv [1] 2-214.

CONTENTS, Volume I: p. [i] title-page. p. [ii] The Facilities Given In This Work. p. [iii] Dedication. p. [iv] *two woodcuts*. p. [v] Address to School-Masters & Parents. p. [vii] *centered on the page with a rule above and beneath, a quotation from Cicero with English translation*. p. [viii] Opinions in Favour of the Present Plan of Teaching. (pp. ix-x *missing*) p. xi *Opinion 5*. p. xii The Only Objection to Our Virgil Answered. p. [1] Contents. p. v Preface. p. [1] A Discourse on Pastoral Poetry, By Alexander Pope. p. 5 First Pastoral. p. 13 Imitation of Eclogue I. p. 19 Second Pastoral. p. 31 Imitations of Eclogue II. p. 39 Third Pastoral. p. 66 Imitations of Eclogue III. p. 79 Fourth Pastoral. p. 117 Imitations of Eclogue IV.

TITLE-PAGE, Volume II: Identical to Volume I, except for the changed volume number.

COLLATION: 12°: π² U-3D⁶ 3E² : 190 leaves + 40 leaves bearing illustrations.

PAGINATION: [2pp.] 215-592.

CONTENTS: [2pp.] title-page + *blank* verso. p. 215 Fifth Pastoral. p. 285 Imitations of Eclogue V. p. 357 Sixth Pastoral. p. 453 Seventh Pastoral. p. 479 Eighth Pastoral. p. 503 Eighth Pastoral, Second Part. p. 531 Ninth Pastoral. p. 557 Imitation of Eclogue IX. p. 563 Tenth Pastoral. p. 587 Imitation of Eclogue X. p. 592 Concluding Remark.

NOTE: Imprint on last page: Stereotyped and Printed by D. Cock and Co. 75, Dean Street, Soho, London.

PLATES

Among the 69 leaves with illustrations, 17 wood engravings were designed and executed by Blake. Except for no. 1 below, the designs are printed 4 to a page. The impressions are very poor in many copies. All words printed with the designs are type set and are not part of the woodblocks themselves. Sets of proof sheets of nos. 2-5 and 6-9, printed before the blocks were trimmed for publication, are in the Rosenwald Collection, the BM Department of Prints and Drawings, and the Fitzwilliam Museum (second sheet only, inserted in the manuscript of *An Island in the Moon*). The first of these two sheets from the Rosenwald Collection is reproduced here. The BM copies of these proofs are reproduced in Geoffrey Keynes, *Bibliography of William Blake*, facing p. 212, Keynes, *William Blake's Engravings* (London, 1950), pls. 116, 117, and *The Illustrations of William Blake for Thornton's Virgil*, with an intro. by Keynes (London, 1937). This last work also contains a set of prints from electrotypes of the woodblocks printed one to a sheet. The original woodblocks are now in the BM Department of Prints and Drawings.

Keynes, *The Illustrations of William Blake for Thornton's Virgil*, contains reproductions of the preliminary sketches of nos. 2-4, 6, 8-11, 13, 14, 16, and 17 and for one design never engraved. These sketches, now all dispersed to various owners, are also reproduced in Keynes, *Pencil Drawings by William Blake* (London, 1927), pls. 50-54. The drawing for no. 7, not included among the Keynes reproductions, is reproduced in [Edwin Wolf 2nd and Elizabeth Mongan, compilers], *William Blake 1757-1827: A Descriptive Catalogue of an Exhibition of the Works of William Blake Selected from Collections in the United States* (Philadelphia, 1939), p. 85.

Several impressions were taken from the woodblocks in the nineteenth century by the Linnell family and trustees. Sets of these so-called "proofs" are in the HEH and the Doheny Library, St. John's Seminary, Camarillo, California. A set of proofs printed "from the original wood blocks" in 1937 is listed in *Bibliotheca Bibliographici*, A Catalogue of the Library Formed by Geoffrey Keynes (London, 1964), item 600.

Three wood engravings in the series illustrating the "Imitation of Eclogue I" were executed by another hand after Blake's designs. A fourth wood engraving was cut by Byfield after a drawing by Blake which is itself based on a design by Poussin. Six copper-plate intaglio engravings of classical busts and coins are signed by Blake as designer and engraver, but are clearly based on the work of another (at the very least the sculptor of the busts). All of these designs will be reproduced in Volume III of this publication.

1. Vol. I, facing p. 13.
   PRINTED above the design: To face page 13. | ILLUSTRATIONS | OF | IMITATION OF ECLOGUE I. | FRONTISPIECE.
   PRINTED below the design: THENOT AND COLINET. | [rule] | The Illustrations of this English Pastoral are by the famous | BLAKE, the illustrator of *Young's* Night Thoughts, and *Blair's* | Grave; who designed and engraved them himself. This is men- | tioned, as they display less of art than genius, and are much | admired by some eminent painters.
   DESIGN SIZE: 6.1 × 8.5 cm.

2. Vol. I, facing p. 14, top design.
   PRINTED above the design: To face page 14. | ILLUSTRATIONS OF IMITATION OF ECLOGUE I.

PRINTED below the design: COLINET.
DESIGN SIZE: 3.7 × 7.5 cm.

3. Vol. I, facing p. 14, second design from the top.
PRINTED below the design: THENOT.
DESIGN SIZE: 3.2 × 7.5 cm.
   NOTE: An impression from the original woodblock is printed in *The Athenaeum*, no. 795 (Jan. 21, 1843), 65.

4. Vol. I, facing p. 14, third design from the top.
PRINTED below the design: COLINET and THENOT.
DESIGN SIZE: 3.3 × 7.4 cm.

5. Vol. I, facing p. 14, bottom design.
PRINTED below the design: COLINET.
DESIGN SIZE: 3.6 × 7.5 cm.
   NOTE: An impression from the original woodblock is printed in Alexander Gilchrist, *Life of William Blake* (London & Cambridge, 1863), I, 271 and (London, 1880), I, facing p. 320.

6. Vol. I, facing p. 15, top design.
PRINTED above the design: To face page 15. | ILLUSTRATIONS OF IMITATION OF ECLOGUE I.
PRINTED below the design: THENOT.
DESIGN SIZE: 3.4 × 7.4 cm.
   NOTE: An impression from the original woodblock is printed in Alexander Gilchrist, *Life of William Blake* (London & Cambridge, 1863), I, 271 and (London, 1880), I, facing p. 320.

7. Vol. I, facing p. 15, second design from the top.
PRINTED below the design: THENOT.
DESIGN SIZE: 3.5 × 7.4 cm.

8. Vol. I, facing p. 15, third design from the top.
PRINTED below the design: COLINET.
DESIGN SIZE: 3.3 × 7.4 cm.

9. Vol. I, facing p. 15, bottom design.
PRINTED below the design: COLINET.
DESIGN SIZE: 3.6 × 7.5 cm.
   NOTE: An impression from the original woodblock is printed in Alexander Gilchrist, *Life of William Blake* (London & Cambridge, 1863), I, 271 and (London, 1880), I, facing p. 320.

10. Vol. I, p. 16, top design.
PRINTED above the design: To face page 16. | ILLUSTRATIONS OF IMITATION OF ECLOGUE I.
PRINTED below the design: THENOT.
DESIGN SIZE: 3.2 × 7.8 cm.

11. Vol. I, facing p. 16, second design from the top.

PRINTED below the design: COLINET.
DESIGN SIZE: 3.2 × 7.6 cm.

12. Vol. I, facing p. 16, third design from the top.
PRINTED below the design: COLINET.
DESIGN SIZE: 3.5 × 7.8 cm.

13. Vol. I, facing p. 16, bottom design.
PRINTED below the design: THENOT.
DESIGN SIZE: 3.5 × 7.8 cm.

14. Vol. I, facing p. 18, top design.
PRINTED above the design: To face page 18. | ILLUSTRATIONS OF IMITATION OF ECLOGUE I.
PRINTED below the design: THENOT. To illustrate lines 1, 2.
DESIGN SIZE: 3.6 × 7.7 cm.

15. Vol. I, facing p. 18, second design from the top.
PRINTED below the design: 3, 4, 5, 6.
DESIGN SIZE: 3.5 × 7.7 cm.

16. Vol. I, facing p. 18, third design from the top.
PRINTED below the design: 7, 8, 9.
DESIGN SIZE: 3.5 × 7.8 cm.

17. Vol. I, facing p. 18, bottom design.
PRINTED below the design: 10.
DESIGN SIZE: 3.3 × 7.8 cm.

COPIES EXAMINED: GEB (2, one lacking the wood engravings listed above and one of the first vol. only); HEH; I; P (2); RNE (first vol. only).

COPIES REPRODUCED: P (pls. 1-17); R (first proof sheet).

Russell #30; Keynes #77; Binyon #137-153; Bentley & Nurmi #411.

XI. REMEMBER ME! 1825 & 1826.

TITLE-PAGE: The first edition, 1825, engraved and therefore reproduced as pl. XI, 2.

COLLATION: 12°: b^{12} B-P^{12} Q-S^6: 198 leaves + 21 plates. 13.2 × 8.5 cm.

PAGINATION: [i] ii-iv [v] vi-xxiv [1] 2-11 [12] 13-336 + [24pp.] 361-364.

CONTENTS: [engraved title-page]. p. [i] Contents. p. [v] Introduction. Selico and Berissa, An African Story. By Doctor Thornton. p. [1] St. Aubin and Angelina. By Miss Silvia Thornton. p. [12] A Singular Instance of Sympathy. By Dr. Gillies. p. 32 The Hiding of Moses. p. 35 Lord Thurlow. p. 36 The Bachelor's Choice. p. 37 Recommendation to Instructors of Youth to Persevere. p. 38 Account of the Moravian Converts at the Cape of Good Hope. From Barrow's Travels. p. 41 On the Exalted Faculties of Man. p. 42 The Snowdrop. By Doctor Thornton. p. 44 Imposition on the Pope, and on Kircher the Antiquarian. p. 45 Address to the Supreme. By Miss Elizabeth Carter. p. 47 Lines for a Lady's Pocket Book. [signed] Chris. Smart. p. 48 Origin of the Saying, "A Cock and a Bull Story." p. 49 Objects of the Mind. p. 51 Contrast Between Christ and Mahomet. p. 52 To My Nightcap. p. 53 Value of Education, Exemplified by the Diamond. p. 54 The Oyster. p. 55 Of the Learned Ladies In Italy. By Dr. Cocchi. p. 56 The Lawyer's Prayer. By Judge Blackstone. p. 57 Honours Conferred Upon Woman by the Romans. p. 60 Epigram on Sir Joshua Reynolds. p. 61 The Man of Ross. p. 62 Watches. p. 63 Lachin Y Gair. By Lord Byron. p. 65 Silent Glances. [signed] M.A. p. 66 The Sea-boy's Dream. p. 67 Secretary Addison and the Young Duke of Warton. By Young, the Poet. p. 68 The Sheperd's Dream. By Robert Bloomfield. p. 71 Account of a Quaker's Meeting. By Mr. Spence. p. 72 Origin of the Word Tyburn. p. 73 Botany for Ladies. By Doctor Thornton. p. 88 On Flower Painting. p. 93 On Grouping. p. 94 On the Rose. [signed] Cardinal De Bernis. p. 94 Story of the Persian Heroine; or, Downfall of Tyranny, and Triumph of Female Virtue, by Miss Thornton. [a play]. p. 116 Song. p. 117 The Death of Hafed and Hinda. From Lalla Rooksh. p. 123 King George II. and His People. p. 124 To a Child, by Joanna Baillie. p. 125 Death of Squire Armitage. p. 127 Sonnet. Written at Midnight. [signed] R.A. Davenport. p. 128 Account of Wycherly's Marriage with Lady Drogheda. By Dennis. p. 129 British Feeling. p. 130 Translation from Horace. By Miss Carter. p. 131 Stanzas on Life. p. 132 Translation from Horace. By Miss Carter. p. 133 Dryden. p. 134 On A Distant View of the Village and School of Harrow on the Hill. By Lord Byron. p. 135 Doctor Busby and His Scholars. p. 136 Conduct of Cromwell after the Decapitation of Charles I. p. 136 Discovery of the Body of King Charles I. in Windsor Chapel. p. 138 Why Cromwell put King Charles the First to Death. p. 139 Compliment Paid to a Ham, by Doctor Meredith. p. 140 George II. and the Quack Doctor Ward. p. 142 Tribute of the Stage to the Memory of Princess Charlotte. p. 144 Monody Written by Thomas Campbell, Esq. and Spoken by Miss Bartley. p. 147 How

Marriages are Contracted in Egypt. p. 148 Night Blowing Cereus; or, Torch Thistle. By Doctor Thornton. p. 149 Renealmia Nutans; or, Nodding Renealmia. By Doctor Thornton. p. 150 Sheridan and His Wine Merchant. p. 151 Leonardo Da Vinci and The Prior. p. 152 Wit of Charles Fox. p. 153 Anecdote of Salvator Rosa. By Lady Morgan. p. 154 Conlath and Cuthona. A Poem. By Ossian. Son of Fingal. p. 160 On the Death of the Poet Byron. By Doctor Thornton. p. 167 How Colds and Inflammatory Fevers are Caught. p. 174 Funeral Oration on Lord Byron. Delivered by Spiridion Tricoupi. p. 181 Funeral of Lord Byron. p. 182 Life of Ali Pacha. p. 187 Absence from Her We Love. From "The Star in the East." p. 189 Oracle at Delphos. p. 191 Lines Addressed to Lady Byron. p. 193 Farewell to England. p. 203 Excuse of a Chorister who could not sing. p. 204 Houses in Turkey. p. 205 Manner of Dining Amongst the Persians. p. 207 Lines on a Female Warrior Killed in Palestine. p. 209 Superstition and Priestcraft. By the Rev. J. Connor, Missionary. p. 214 Anecdote of a Clergyman. p. 215 John Wesley and General Oglethorp. p. 216 Life and Sufferings of Mrs. Anne Ayscough. p. 237 An Elegy. p. 238 Lord Elliot and a Young Officer. p. 239 Meeting of James King of Scotland and the Lady of the Lake. By Sir Walter Scott, BART. p. 249 Sonnet. p. 250 Origin of Bands. p. 253 Bisset and His Animals. p. 256 Henry Lee Warner, Esq. p. 258 Seers. p. 259 College Barber. p. 260 Necromancy. By Captain Parry. p. 262 The Barber and the Cat. p. 263 Fortitude of an American Indian. p. 266 Anecdote of the Rev. Geo. Harvest. p. 267 Belief of the Indians in Dreams. p. 268 Wanderer from Erin. By Thomas Campbell. p. 269 Perplexity of a Moderator. p. 270 On the Sagacity of the American Indian as Respects Travelling. p. 273 To a Lady, With Some Painted Flowers. p. 274 The Rescue; or Story of Raymond and Ellenor. By Miss Thornton. With a Plate by Linnell. p. 285 Fate of Castelard, The Lover of Mary Queen of Scots. p. 286 A Rake Reformed; or History of the Duke of Castellamore and Rosalba. By Miss Thornton. p. 300 Love Discovered. p. 301 Bathmendi, A Persian Story. By Miss Thornton. p. 323 Death of Ali Pacha. p. 324 Lines on Greece. By Doctor Thornton. p. 325 The National Tiger. p. 325 Song. p. 326 The Dragon Arum. By Doctor Thornton. p. 327 Artful Decision of Cardinal Spada. p. 327 An Epitaph. p. 328 Gleaning after Harvest. p. 329 To the Rose. By Lord Thurlow. p. 331 Swift's Letter to Pope. p. 332 Singular Interposition of Providence in Favour of the Protestants in Ireland. p. 333 Home Is Still Home However Homely. p. 334 Simple Nature; or the Two Young Mothers. By a Spectator. [8 pp. of engraved plates of music: p. 1 Le Rousseau. p. 2 La Troubadour. p. 4 La Belle Swisse. p. 6 Le Portrait. p. 7 La Tivoli. p. 8 L' Anglaisse.] *engraved sectional title-page:* KALENDAR | and | ALBUM | 1825 | Dedicated | to | *FRIENDSHIP* | and Superior Intellect. | 4 *ff.* [24 pp. *note paper with ruled frames.*] p. 361 Bankers in London and Westminister. p. 363 Terms and Returns in 1825. p. 364 Holidays. | Transfer Days. p. [365] Sovereign Princes of Europe, with their British Marriages and Issue. p. 372 Courts of Law.

TITLE-PAGE, the second edition, 1826: Identical except the date is altered.

COLLATION: 12°: π^4 b^{12} B-P^{12}: 184 leaves + 21 plates.

PAGINATION: [8 pp.] [i] ii-iv [v] vi-xxiv [1] 2-11 [12] 13-336.

CONTENTS: Identical to the 1825 edition except that the changed Kalendar for 1826 now follows the engraved title-page, and the blank pages with ruled frames are omitted. The reference material found in the first edition on pp. 361-372 is also omitted.

PLATES

Twenty-one plates, one of which is an intaglio copper-plate engraving designed and executed by Blake.

1. Facing p. 32, with lower margin bound in.
   INSCRIPTION lower right: *Blake del et sculpt.*
   INSCRIPTION below design: *Hiding of Moses.*
   DESIGN SIZE: 6.8 × 9.8 cm. The inscription is .7 cm. below the design.
   NOTE: A pre-publication proof impression of this plate in the Rosenwald Collection is reproduced in Geoffrey Keynes, *Blake Studies* (London, 1949), pl. 47 and (Oxford, 1971), pl. 39. In the proof, measuring 7 × 11.1 cm., the lower and left margins are larger, with several more small buildings showing on the left. The proof is inscribed "*W Blake. inven. & sculp.*" below the design on the right and "*The Hiding of Moses*" below the design. The water color version of the design is described and reproduced in C. H. Collins Baker, *Catalogue of William Blake's Drawings and Paintings in the Huntington Library,* Enlarged and Revised by R. R. Wark (San Marino, Calif., 1957), pp. 37-38 and pl. XXVIII. Russell (p. 102) speculates that the water color is a replica of a lost tempera painting, described in Alexander Gilchrist, *Life of William Blake* (London & Cambridge, 1863), II, 224, no. 114 and (London, 1880), II, 235, no. 137.

COPIES EXAMINED: HEH (loose pl. mounted in the Kitto Bible, vol. LX, p. 10822); P; W (first and second eds.).
COPY REPRODUCED: P.
Russell #32; Keynes #78; Binyon #104; Bentley & Nurmi #400.

THE PLATES

I. *The Royal Universal Family Bible*, pl. 1

II. Thomas Commins, *An Elegy set to Music*, pl. 1.
    [Plate reduced]

II. Commins, engraved title-page. pl. 2
   [Plate reduced]

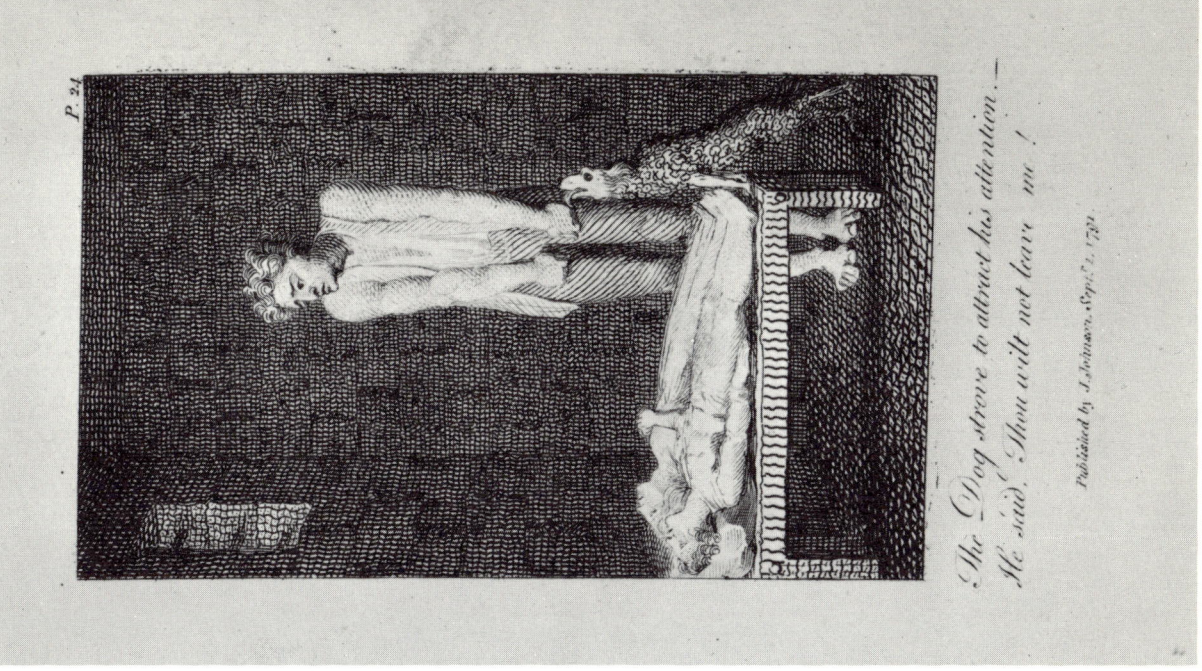

III. Mary Wollstonecraft, *Original Stories from Real Life.* pl. 1B (second state)

III. pl. 2B (second state)

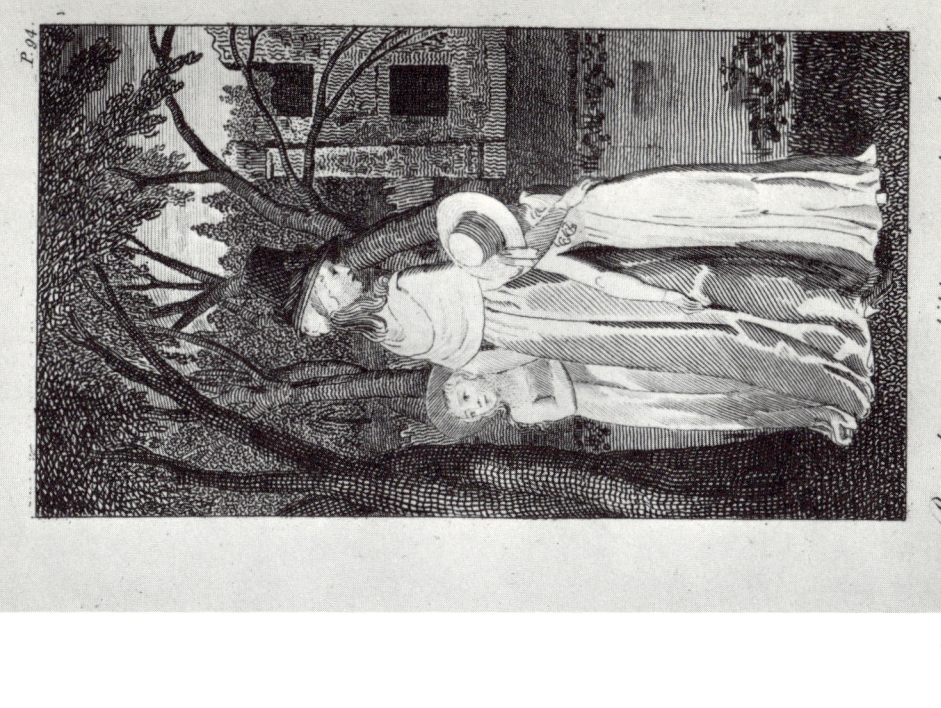

III. pl. 4A

III. pl. 3A

Œconomy & Self-denial are necessary, in every station, to enable us to be generous.

Published by J. Johnson. Sept'r 1, 1791.

III. pl. 6A

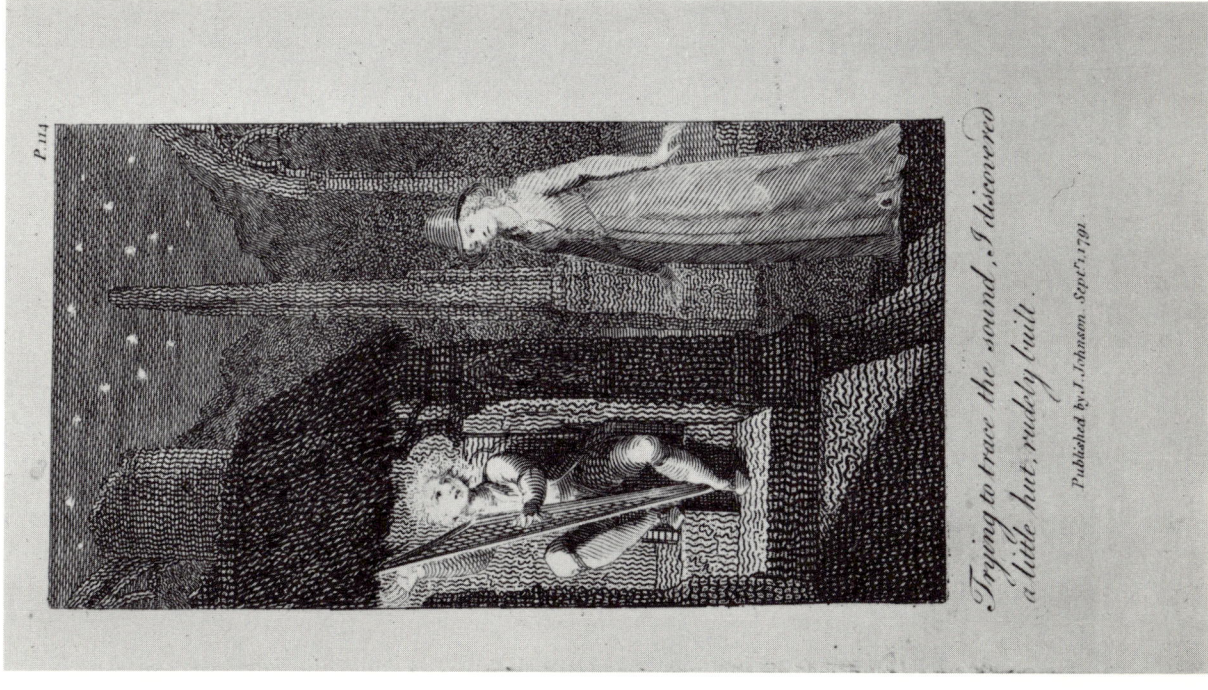

Trying to trace the sound, I discovered a little hut, rudely built.

Published by J. Johnson. Sept'r 1, 1791.

III. pl. 5A

IV. Edward Young, *The Complaint, and The Consolation; or Night Thoughts*. pl. 1
[The plates are substantially reduced]

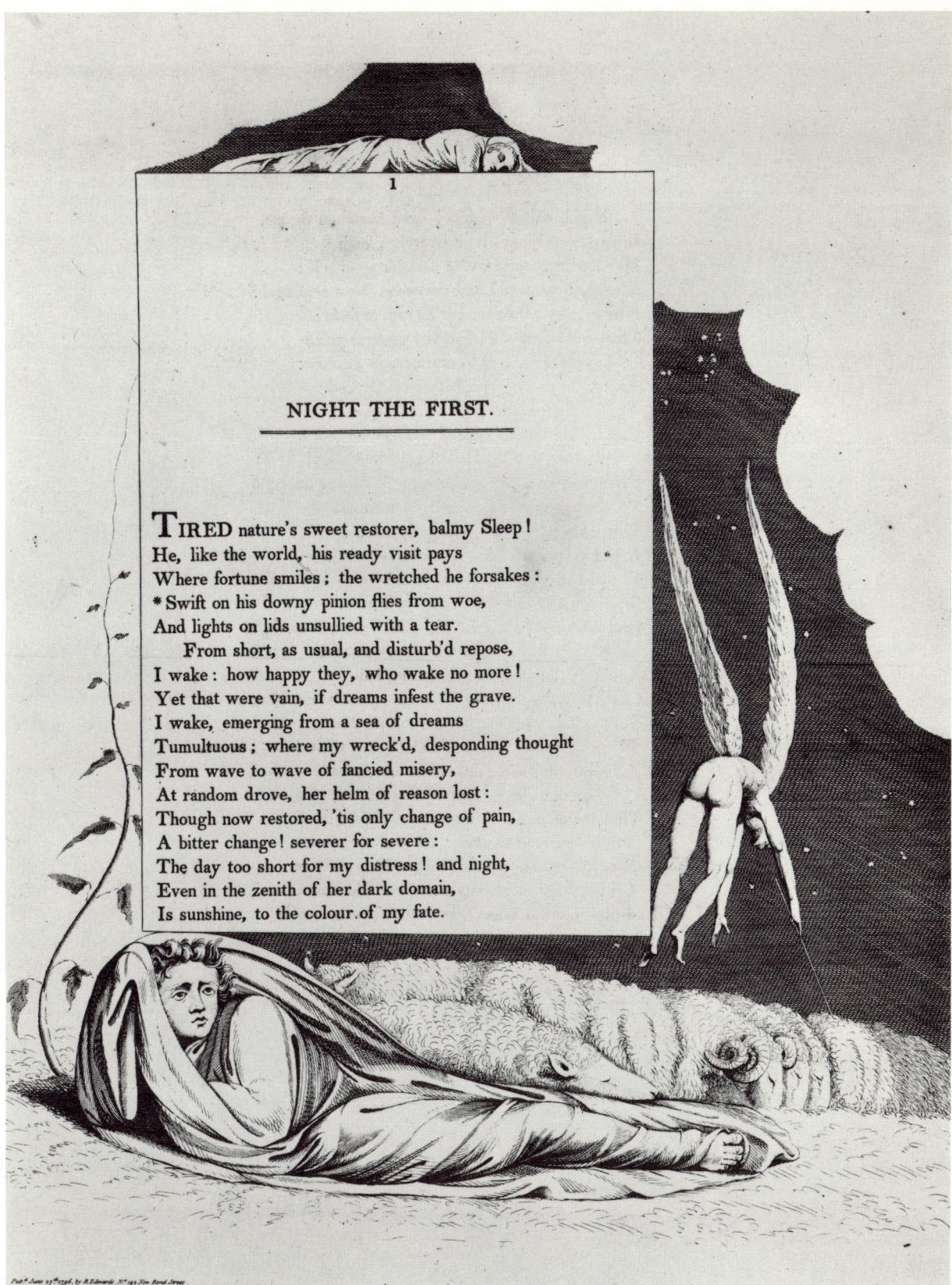

NIGHT THE FIRST.

TIRED nature's sweet restorer, balmy Sleep!
He, like the world, his ready visit pays
Where fortune smiles; the wretched he forsakes:
* Swift on his downy pinion flies from woe,
And lights on lids unsullied with a tear.
    From short, as usual, and disturb'd repose,
I wake: how happy they, who wake no more!
Yet that were vain, if dreams infest the grave.
I wake, emerging from a sea of dreams
Tumultuous; where my wreck'd, desponding thought
From wave to wave of fancied misery,
At random drove, her helm of reason lost:
Though now restored, 'tis only change of pain,
A bitter change! severer for severe:
The day too short for my distress! and night,
Even in the zenith of her dark domain,
Is sunshine, to the colour of my fate.

IV. pl. 3

7

How richly were my noontide trances hung
With gorgeous tapestries of pictured joys,
Joy behind joy, in endless perspective!
* Till at Death's toll, whose restless iron tongue
Calls daily for his millions at a meal,
Starting I 'woke, and found myself undone.
Where's now my frenzy's pompous furniture?
The cobweb'd cottage, with its ragged wall
Of mould'ring mud, is royalty to me:
The spider's most attenuated thread,
Is cord, is cable, to man's tender tie
On earthly bliss; it breaks at every breeze.
    O ye blest scenes of permanent delight!
Full, above measure! lasting, beyond bound!
A perpetuity of bliss, is bliss.
Could you, so rich in rapture, fear an end,
That ghastly thought would drink up all your joy,
And quite unparadise the realms of light.
Safe are you lodged above these rolling spheres;
The baleful influence of whose giddy dance
Sheds sad vicissitude on all beneath.
Here teems with revolutions every hour,
And rarely for the better; or the best,
More mortal than the common births of fate:
Each moment has its sickle, emulous
Of time's enormous scythe, whose ample sweep
Strikes empires from the root; each moment plays
His little weapon in the narrower sphere
Of sweet domestick comfort, and cuts down
The fairest bloom of sublunary bliss.

IV. pl. 4

8

    Bliss! sublunary bliss!—proud words, and vain!
Implicit treason to divine decree!
A bold invasion of the rights of heaven!
I clasp'd the phantoms, and I found them air:
O had I weigh'd it ere my fond embrace,
What darts of agony had miss'd my heart!
* Death! great proprietor of all! 'tis thine
To tread out empire, and to quench the stars:
The sun himself by thy permission shines;
And, one day, thou shalt pluck him from his sphere.
Amidst such mighty plunder, why exhaust
Thy partial quiver on a mark so mean?
Why thy peculiar rancour wreak'd on me?
Insatiate archer! could not one suffice?
Thy shaft flew thrice—and thrice my peace was slain;
And thrice, ere thrice yon moon had fill'd her horn.
O Cynthia! why so pale? dost thou lament
Thy wretched neighbour? grieve to see thy wheel
Of ceaseless change outwhirl'd in human life?
How wanes my borrow'd bliss from fortune's smile!
Precarious courtesy! not virtue's sure,
Self-given, solar ray of sound delight.
    In every varied posture, place, and hour,
How widow'd every thought of every joy!
Thought, busy thought! too busy for my peace,
Through the dark postern of time long elapsed,
Led softly; by the stillness of the night,
Led like a murderer, and such it proves;
Strays, wretched rover! o'er the pleasing past;
In quest of wretchedness perversely strays;

IV. pl. 5

10

What numbers, once in fortune's lap high-fed,
Solicit the cold hand of charity—
To shock us more—solicit it in vain!
Ye silken sons of pleasure! since in pains
You rue more modish visits, visit here,
And breathe from your debauch: give, and reduce
Surfeit's dominion o'er you—but so great
Your impudence, you blush at what is right.
    Happy! did sorrow seize on such alone:
Not prudence can defend, or virtue save:
* Disease invades the chastest temperance,
And punishment the guiltless; and alarm,
Through thickest shades pursues the fond of peace.
Man's caution often into danger turns,
And, his guard falling, crushes him to death.
Not happiness itself makes good her name;
Our very wishes give us not our wish:
How distant oft the thing we doat on most,
From that for which we doat, felicity!
The smoothest course of nature has its pains;
And truest friends, through error, wound our rest.
Without misfortune—what calamities!
And what hostilities—without a foe!
Nor are foes wanting to the best on earth:
But endless is the list of human ills,
And sighs might sooner fail, than cause to sigh.
    A part how small of the terraqueous globe
Is tenanted by man! the rest a waste;
Rocks, deserts, frozen seas, and burning sands—
Wild haunts of monsters, poisons, stings, and death:

IV. pl. 6

12

But rises in demand for her delay;
She makes a scourge of past prosperity
To sting thee more, and double thy distress.
    LORENZO, fortune makes her court to thee;
Thy fond heart dances, while the syren sings:
Dear is thy welfare; think me not unkind,
I would not damp, but to secure thy joys:
Think not that fear is sacred to the storm;
Stand on thy guard against the smiles of fate.
Is heaven tremendous in its frowns? most sure—
And in its favours formidable too:
* Its favours here are trials, not rewards;
A call to duty, not discharge from care;
And should alarm us, full as much as woes;
Awake us to their cause and consequence;
And make us tremble, weigh'd with our desert.
Awe nature's tumults, and chastise her joys,
Lest, while we clasp, we kill them; nay, invert
To worse than simple misery their charms:
Revolted joys, like foes in civil war,
Like bosom friendships to resentment sour'd,
With rage envenom'd rise against our peace.
Beware what earth calls happiness; beware
All joys, but joys that never can expire:
Who builds on less than an immortal base,
Fond as he seems, condemns his joys to death.
    Mine died with thee, PHILANDER! thy last sigh
Dissolved the charm; the disenchanted earth
Lost all her lustre: where her glitt'ring towers?
Her golden mountains where?—all darken'd down

IV. pl. 7

13

To naked waste; a dreary vale of tears:
The great magician's dead! thou poor pale piece
Of outcast earth—in darkness! what a change
From yesterday! thy darling hope so near,
Long-labour'd prize, O how ambition flush'd
Thy glowing cheek! ambition, truly great,
Of virtuous praise: death's subtle seed within,
Sly, treacherous miner! working in the dark,
Smiled at thy well-concerted scheme, and beckon'd
The worm to riot on that rose so red,
Unfaded ere it fell—one moment's prey!
    Man's foresight is conditionally wise;
LORENZO! wisdom into folly turns
Oft, the first instant its idea fair
To lab'ring thought is born: how dim our eye!
* The present moment terminates our sight;
Clouds, thick as those on doomsday, drown the next;
We penetrate, we prophesy in vain:
Time is dealt out by particles; and each,
Ere mingled with the streaming sands of life,
By fate's inviolable oath is sworn
Deep silence, " where eternity begins."
    By nature's law, what may be, may be now;
There's no prerogative in human hours:
In human hearts what bolder thought can rise,
Than man's presumption on to-morrow's dawn?
Where is to-morrow?—in another world!
For numbers this is certain; the reverse
Is sure to none; and yet on this perhaps,
This peradventure—infamous for lies,

15

The thing they can't but purpose, they postpone:
'Tis not in folly, not to scorn a fool;
And scarce in human wisdom to do more:
All promise is poor dilatory man,
And that through every stage: when young, indeed,
In full content we sometimes nobly rest,
Unanxious for ourselves; and only wish,
As duteous sons, our fathers were more wise:
At thirty man suspects himself a fool;
Knows it at forty, and reforms his plan;
At fifty chides his infamous delay,
Pushes his prudent purpose to resolve;
In all the magnanimity of thought
Resolves, and re-resolves; then dies the same.
    And why? because he thinks himself immortal:
All men think all men mortal, but themselves;
Themselves;—when some alarming shock of fate
Strikes through their wounded hearts the sudden dread;
But their hearts wounded, like the wounded air,
Soon close; where pass'd the shaft no trace is found.
As from the wing no scar the sky retains;
The parted wave no furrow from the keel;
So dies in human hearts the thought of death:
Even with the tender tear which nature sheds
O'er those we love, we drop it in their grave.
Can I forget PHILANDER? that were strange:
O my full heart!—but should I give it vent,
* The longest night though longer far, would fail,
And the lark listen to my midnight song.

IV. pl. 9

16

The sprightly lark's shrill matin wakes the morn,
Grief's sharpest thorn hard pressing on my breast;
I strive, with wakeful melody, to cheer
The sullen gloom, sweet philomel! like thee,
And call the stars to listen; every star
Is deaf to mine, enamour'd of thy lay:
Yet be not vain; there are, who thine excel,
And charm through distant ages: wrapp'd in shade,
Pris'ner of darkness! to the silent hours,
How often I repeat their rage divine,
To lull my griefs, and steal my heart from woe!
I roll their raptures, but not catch their fire:
Dark, though not blind, like thee Mæonides!
Or, Milton! thee; ah, could I reach your strain!
Or his, who made Mæonides our own:
Man too he sung—immortal man I sing:
* Oft bursts my song beyond the bounds of life;
What now, but immortality, can please?
O had he press'd his theme, pursued the track,
Which opens out of darkness into day!
O had he mounted on his wing of fire,
Soar'd, where I sink, and sung immortal man!
How had it bless'd mankind, and rescued me!

IV. pl. 10

NIGHT THE SECOND.

"WHEN the cock crew, he wept"—smote by that eye
Which looks on me, on all; that power, who bids
This midnight centinel, with clarion shrill,
* Emblem of that which shall awake the dead,
Rouse souls from slumber into thoughts of heaven:
Shall I too weep? where then is fortitude?
And, fortitude abandon'd, where is man?
I know the terms on which he sees the light;
He that is born, is listed; life is war,
Eternal war with woe: who bears it best,
Deserves it least—on other themes I'll dwell.
LORENZO! let me turn my thoughts on thee,
And thine, on themes may profit; profit there,
Where most thy need—themes, too, the genuine growth
Of dear PHILANDER's dust: he, thus, though dead,
May still befriend.—What themes? time's wondrous price,
Death, friendship, and PHILANDER's final scene.

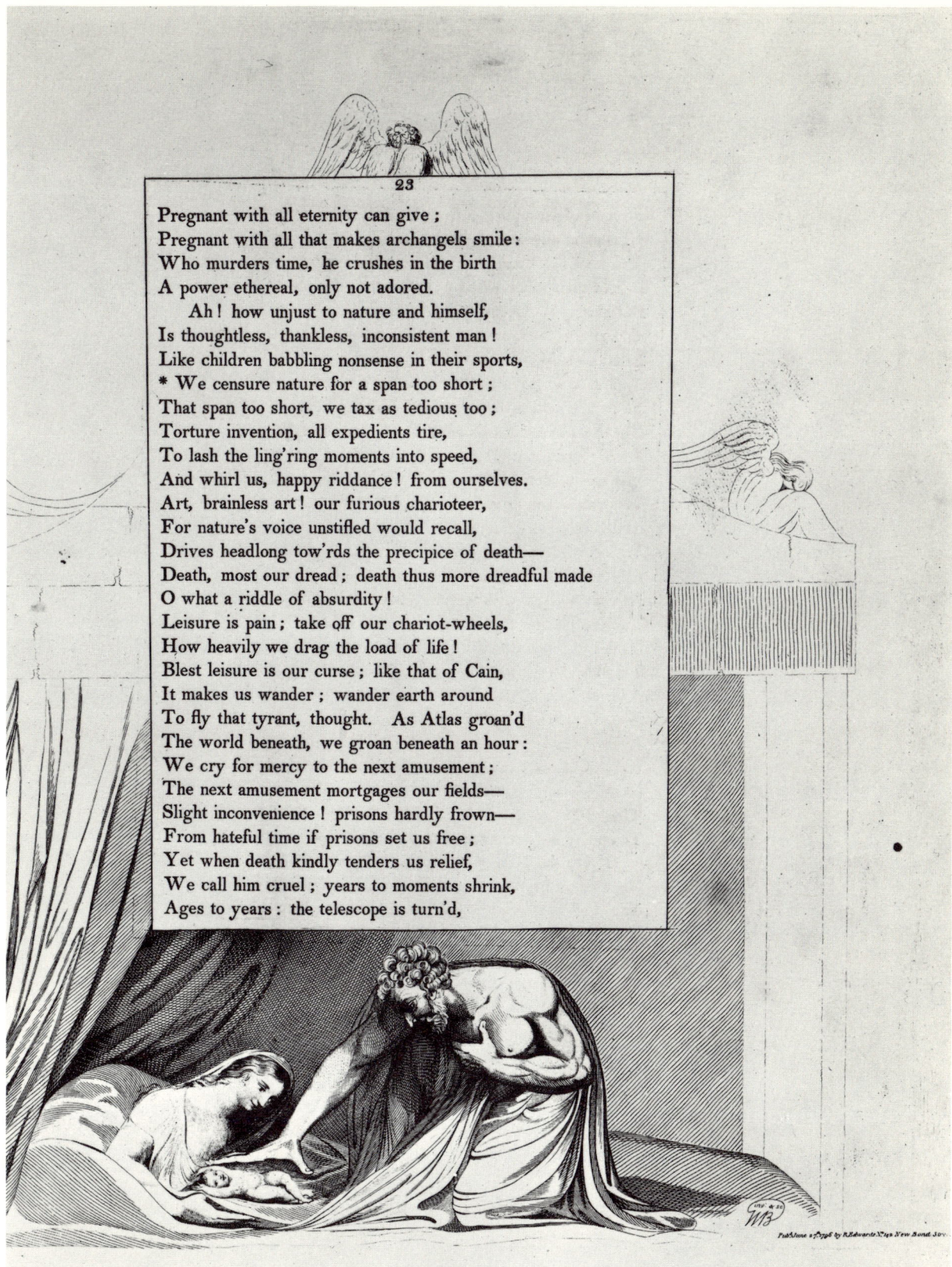

23

Pregnant with all eternity can give;
Pregnant with all that makes archangels smile:
Who murders time, he crushes in the birth
A power ethereal, only not adored.

    Ah! how unjust to nature and himself,
Is thoughtless, thankless, inconsistent man!
Like children babbling nonsense in their sports,
* We censure nature for a span too short;
That span too short, we tax as tedious too;
Torture invention, all expedients tire,
To lash the ling'ring moments into speed,
And whirl us, happy riddance! from ourselves.
Art, brainless art! our furious charioteer,
For nature's voice unstifled would recall,
Drives headlong tow'rds the precipice of death—
Death, most our dread; death thus more dreadful made
O what a riddle of absurdity!
Leisure is pain; take off our chariot-wheels,
How heavily we drag the load of life!
Blest leisure is our curse; like that of Cain,
It makes us wander; wander earth around
To fly that tyrant, thought. As Atlas groan'd
The world beneath, we groan beneath an hour:
We cry for mercy to the next amusement;
The next amusement mortgages our fields—
Slight inconvenience! prisons hardly frown—
From hateful time if prisons set us free;
Yet when death kindly tenders us relief,
We call him cruel; years to moments shrink,
Ages to years: the telescope is turn'd,

IV. pl. 13

IV. pl. 14

25

We thwart the DEITY; and 'tis decreed,
Who thwart his will shall contradict their own:
Hence our unnatural quarrel with ourselves;
Our thoughts at enmity; our bosom-broil:
We push time from us, and we wish him back;
Lavish of lustrums, and yet fond of life;
Life we think long, and short; death seek, and shun;
Body and soul, like peevish man and wife,
United jar, and yet are loth to part.
    Oh the dark days of vanity! while here,
How tasteless! and how terrible when gone!
Gone! they ne'er go; when past, they haunt us still;
The spirit walks of every day deceased;
And smiles an angel, or a fury frowns:
Nor death, nor life delight us—if time past,
And time possess'd, both pain us, what can please?
That which the DEITY to please ordain'd—
Time used: the man who consecrates his hours
By vigorous effort and an honest aim,
At once he draws the sting of life and death;
He walks with nature—and her paths are peace.
    Our error's cause and cure are seen: see next
Time's nature, origin, importance, speed;
And thy great gain from urging his career.
All-sensual man, because untouch'd, unseen,
He looks on time as nothing: nothing else
Is truly man's; 'tis fortune's—Time's a God:
Hast thou ne'er heard of time's omnipotence?
For, or against, what wonders can he do—
And will! to stand blank neuter he disdains.

IV. pl. 15

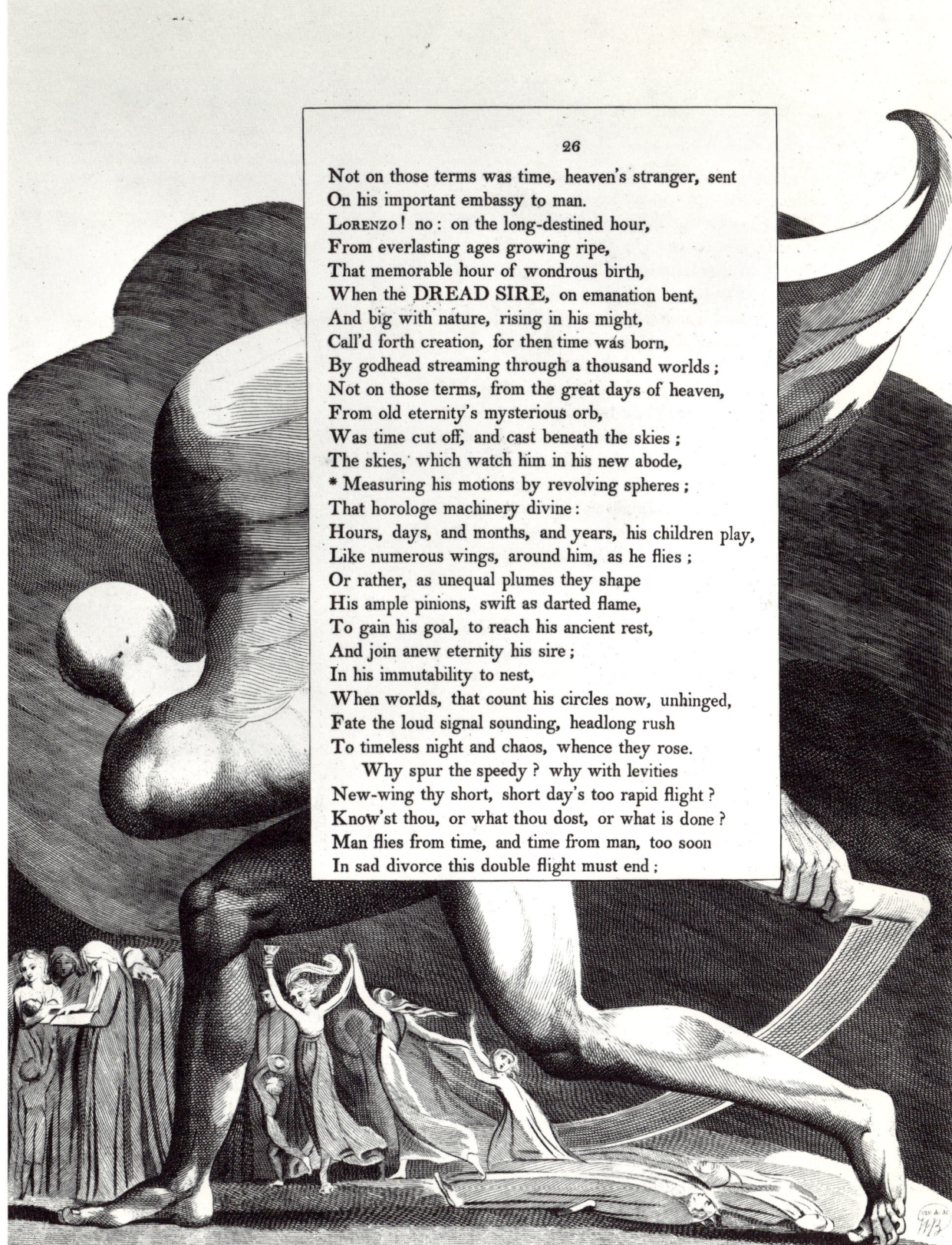

26

Not on those terms was time, heaven's stranger, sent
On his important embassy to man.
LORENZO! no: on the long-destined hour,
From everlasting ages growing ripe,
That memorable hour of wondrous birth,
When the DREAD SIRE, on emanation bent,
And big with nature, rising in his might,
Call'd forth creation, for then time was born,
By godhead streaming through a thousand worlds;
Not on those terms, from the great days of heaven,
From old eternity's mysterious orb,
Was time cut off, and cast beneath the skies;
The skies, which watch him in his new abode,
* Measuring his motions by revolving spheres;
That horologe machinery divine:
Hours, days, and months, and years, his children play,
Like numerous wings, around him, as he flies;
Or rather, as unequal plumes they shape
His ample pinions, swift as darted flame,
To gain his goal, to reach his ancient rest,
And join anew eternity his sire;
In his immutability to nest,
When worlds, that count his circles now, unhinged,
Fate the loud signal sounding, headlong rush
To timeless night and chaos, whence they rose.
    Why spur the speedy? why with levities
New-wing thy short, short day's too rapid flight?
Know'st thou, or what thou dost, or what is done?
Man flies from time, and time from man, too soon
In sad divorce this double flight must end;

IV. pl. 16

27

And then, where are we? where, LORENZO, then
Thy sports—thy pomps?—I grant thee, in a state
Not unambitious; in the ruffled shroud,
Thy parian tomb's triumphant arch beneath:
Has death his fopperies? then well may life
Put on her plume, and in her rainbow shine.

    Ye well-array'd! ye lilies of our land!
Ye lilies male! who neither toil, nor spin,
As sister lilies might;—if not so wise
As Solomon, more sumptuous to the sight!
Ye delicate! who nothing can support,
Yourselves most insupportable! for whom
The winter rose must blow, the sun put on
A brighter beam in Leo, silky-soft
Favonius breathe still softer, or be chid;
And other worlds send odours, sauce, and song,
And robes, and notions framed in foreign looms!
O ye LORENZOS of our age! who deem
One moment unamused, a misery
Not made for feeble man; who call aloud
For every bauble, drivell'd o'er by sense,
For rattles and conceits of every cast,
For change of follies and relays of joy,
To drag your patience through the tedious length
Of a short winter's day—say—sages; say
Wit's oracles; say—dreamers of gay dreams;
How will you weather an eternal night,
Where such expedients fail?

    * O treacherous conscience! while she seems to sleep
On rose and myrtle, lull'd with syren song;

IV. pl. 17

31

Heart-buried in the rubbish of the world—
The world, that gulph of souls, immortal souls,
Souls elevate, angelic, wing'd with fire
To reach the distant skies, and triumph there
On thrones, which shall not mourn their masters changed,
Though we from earth; ethereal, they that fell.
Such veneration due, O man! to man.
    Who venerate themselves, the world despise.
For what, gay friend, is this escutcheon'd world,
Which hangs out death in one eternal night?
A night, that glooms us in the noon-tide ray,
And wraps our thought, at banquets, in the shroud.
Life's little stage is a small eminence,
Inch-high the grave above; that home of man,
Where dwells the multitude; we gaze around;
We read their monuments; we sigh; and while
We sigh, we sink; and are what we deplored:
Lamenting, or lamented, all our lot!
    Is death at distance? no: he has been on thee;
And given sure earnest of his final blow.
Those hours, which lately smiled, where are they now?
Pallid to thought, and ghastly! drown'd, all drown'd
In that great deep, which nothing disembogues;
And, dying, they bequeath'd thee small renown:
The rest are on the wing; how fleet their flight!
Already has the fatal train took fire;
A moment, and the world's blown up to thee;
The sun is darkness, and the stars are dust.
    * 'Tis greatly wise to talk with our past hours,
And ask them, what report they bore to heaven;

IV. pl. 18

33

Erewhile high-flush'd with insolence and wine?
* Like that, the dial speaks; and points to thee,
LORENZO! loth to break thy banquet up.
" O man, thy kingdom is departing from thee;
" And, while it lasts, is emptier than my shade."
Its silent language such; nor need'st thou call
Thy magi, to decypher what it means:
Know, like the Median, fate is in thy walls:
Dost ask, how? whence? Belshazzar-like, amazed?
Man's make encloses the sure seeds of death;
Life feeds the murderer: ingrate! he thrives
On her own meal, and then his nurse devours.
　　　But here, LORENZO, the delusion lies;
That solar shadow, as it measures life,
It life resembles too: life speeds away
From point to point, though seeming to stand still:
The cunning fugitive is swift by stealth,
Too subtle is the movement to be seen;
Yet soon man's hour is up, and we are gone.
Warnings point out our danger; gnomons, time:
As these are useless when the sun is set;
So those, but when more glorious reason shines:
Reason should judge in all; in reason's eye,
That sedentary shadow travels hard:
But such our gravitation to the wrong,
So prone our hearts to whisper what we wish,
'Tis later with the wise, than he's aware;
A Wilmington goes slower than the sun;
And all mankind mistake their time of day;
Even age itself: fresh hopes are hourly sown

IV. pl. 19

35

Had thought been all, sweet speech had been denied;
Speech, thought's canal! speech, thought's criterion too!
Thought in the mine may come forth gold or dross;
When coin'd in words, we know its real worth:
If sterling, store it for thy future use;
'Twill buy thee benefit, perhaps renown:
Thought too, deliver'd, is the more possess'd;
* Teaching, we learn; and giving, we retain
The births of intellect; when dumb, forgot.
Speech ventilates our intellectual fire;
Speech burnishes our mental magazine;
Brightens for ornament, and whets for use.
What numbers, sheath'd in erudition, lie
Plunged to the hilts in venerable tomes,
And rusted; who might have borne an edge,
And play'd a sprightly beam, if born to speech!
If born blest heirs to half their mother's tongue!
'Tis thought's exchange, which, like th' alternate push
Of waves conflicting, breaks the learned scum,
And defecates the student's standing pool.
    In contemplation is his proud resource?
'Tis poor as proud: by converse unsustain'd
Rude thought runs wild in contemplation's field:
Converse, the menage, breaks it to the bit
Of due restraint; and emulation's spur
Gives graceful energy, by rivals awed:
'Tis converse qualifies for solitude,
As exercise for salutary rest:
By that untutor'd, contemplation raves;
And nature's fool, by wisdom's is outdone.

Is virtue kindling at a rival fire,
And, emulously rapid in her race.
O the soft enmity ! endearing strife !
This carries friendship to her noon-tide point,
And gives the rivet of eternity.
     From friendship, which outlives my former themes,
Glorious surviver of old time, and death !
From friendship thus, that flower of heavenly seed,
The wise extract earth's most hyblean bliss,
Superior wisdom crown'd with smiling joy.
     But for whom blossoms this elysian flower ?
Abroad they find, who cherish it at home.
LORENZO ! pardon what my love extorts,
An honest love, and not afraid to frown.
Though choice of follies fasten on the great,
None clings more obstinate than fancy fond
That sacred friendship is their easy prey;
Caught by the wafture of a golden lure,
Or fascination of a high-born smile.
Their smiles, the great, and the coquet throw out
For other hearts, tenacious of their own;
And we no less of ours, when such the bait.
Ye fortune's cofferers ! ye powers of wealth !
You do your rent-rolls most felonious wrong,
By taking our attachment to yourselves :
Can gold gain friendship ? impudence of hope !
As well mere man an angel might beget :
* Love, and love only, is the loan for love.
LORENZO ! pride repress ; nor hope to find
A friend, but what has found a friend in thee.

40

By mortal hand—it merits a divine:
* Angels should paint it, angels ever there;
There on a post of honour, and of joy.
    Dare I presume then? but PHILANDER bids,
And glory tempts, and inclination calls:
Yet am I struck; as struck the soul beneath
Aërial groves' impenetrable gloom;
Or in some mighty ruin's solemn shade;
Or gazing by pale lamps on high-born dust
In vaults; thin courts of poor unflatter'd kings!
Or at the midnight altar's hallow'd flame:
It is religion to proceed: I pause——
And enter, awed, the temple of my theme:
Is it his death-bed? no—it is his shrine:
Behold him, there, just rising to a god.
    The chamber, where the good man meets his fate,
Is privileged beyond the common walk
Of virtuous life, quite in the verge of heaven.
Fly, ye profane! if not, draw near with awe,
Receive the blessing, and adore the chance
That threw in this Bethesda your disease;
If unrestored by this, despair your cure:
For here resistless demonstration dwells;
A death-bed's a detecter of the heart;
Here tired dissimulation drops her mask,
Through life's grimace that mistress of the scene!
Here real and apparent are the same—
You see the man; you see his hold on heaven;
If sound his virtue, as PHILANDER's sound.
Heaven waits not the last moment; owns her friends

IV. pl. 22

41

On this side death; and points them out to men:
A lecture silent, but of sovereign power!
To vice, confusion; and to virtue, peace.
    Whatever farce the boastful hero plays,
Virtue alone has majesty in death;
And greater still, the more the tyrant frowns:
PHILANDER! he severely frown'd on thee:
" No warning given—unceremonious fate!
" A sudden rush from life's meridian joys!
" A wrench from all we love—from all we are!
" A restless bed of pain! a plunge opaque
" Beyond conjecture! feeble nature's dread!
" Strong reason's shudder at the dark unknown!
" A sun extinguish'd! a just opening grave!
" And oh! the last—last—what? can words express?
" Thought reach? the last, last—silence of a friend!"
Where are those horrors, that amazement where,
This hideous group of ills, which singly shock?
Demand from man—I thought him man till now.
    Through nature's wreck, through vanquish'd agonies,
Like the stars struggling through this midnight gloom,
What gleams of joy! what more than human peace!
Where, the frail mortal? the poor abject worm?
No, not in death, the mortal to be found.
His conduct is a legacy for all,
Richer than Mammon's for his single heir:
His comforters he comforts; great in ruin,
With unreluctant grandeur gives, not yields
His soul sublime; and closes with his fate.

46

Or if we wish a fourth, it is a friend——
But friends, how mortal! dangerous the desire.
    Take Phœbus to yourselves, ye basking bards!
Inebriate at fair fortune's fountain-head;
And reeling through the wilderness of joy;
* Where sense runs savage broke from reason's chain,
And sings false peace, till smother'd by the pall.
My fortune is unlike; unlike my song;
Unlike the DEITY my song invokes.
I to day's soft-eyed sister pay my court,
Endymion's rival! and her aid implore;
Now first implored in succour to the muse.
    Thou who didst lately borrow Cynthia's form,
And modestly forego thine own! O thou
Who didst thyself, at midnight hours, inspire!
Say, why not Cynthia patroness of song?
As thou her crescent, she thy character
Assumes; still more a goddess by the change.
    Are there demurring wits, who dare dispute
This revolution in the world inspired?
Ye train pierian! to the lunar sphere,
In silent hour address your ardent call
For aid immortal—less her brother's right.
She, with the spheres harmonious, nightly leads
The mazy dance, and hears their matchless strain;
A strain for gods, denied to mortal ear.
Transmit it heard, thou silver queen of heaven!
What title or what name endears thee most?
Cynthia! Cyllene! Phœbe!—or dost hear
With higher gust fair P——d of the skies?

IV. pl. 25

49

And will not the severe excuse a sigh?
Scorn the proud man that is ashamed to weep;
Our tears indulged indeed deserve our shame:
Ye that e'er lost an angel! pity me.
    Soon as the lustre languish'd in her eye,
Dawning a dimmer day on human sight;
And on her cheek, the residence of spring,
Pale omen sat, and scatter'd fears around
On all that saw, and who would cease to gaze
That once had seen? with haste, parental haste
I flew, I snatch'd her from the rigid north,
Her native bed, on which bleak boreas blew,
And bore her nearer to the sun; the sun,
As if the sun could envy, check'd his beam,
Denied his wonted succour, nor with more
Regret beheld her drooping, than the bells
Of lilies! fairest lilies not so fair.
    Queen lilies! and ye painted populace!
Who dwell in fields, and lead ambrosial lives;
In morn and evening dew your beauties bathe,
And drink the sun, which gives your cheeks to glow,
And out-blush, mine excepted, every fair;
You gladlier grew, ambitious of her hand
Which often cropp'd your odours, incense meet
To thought so pure: ye lovely fugitives!
Coëval race with man, for man you smile;
Why not smile at him too? you share indeed
His sudden pass, but not his constant pain.
    So man is made, nought ministers delight
But what his glowing passions can engage;

IV. pl. 26

54

Where darkness, brooding o'er unfinish'd fates
With raven wing incumbent, waits the day,
Dread day! that interdicts all future change!
That subterranean world, that land of ruin!
Fit walk, Lorenzo, for proud human thought!
There let my thought expatiate; and explore
Balsamic truths, and healing sentiments
Of all most wanted, and most welcome here.
For gay Lorenzo's sake, and for thy own
My soul! " The fruits of dying friends survey;
" Expose the vain of life; weigh life and death;
" Give death his eulogy; thy fear subdue;
" And labour that first palm of noble minds—
" A manly scorn of terror from the tomb:"
This harvest reap from thy Narcissa's grave.

  As poets feign'd, from Ajax' streaming blood
Arose, with grief inscribed, a mournful flower;
Let wisdom blossom from my mortal wound.
And first, of dying friends; what fruit from these?
It brings us more than triple aid; an aid
To chase our thoughtlessness, fear, pride, and guilt.

  Our dying friends come o'er us like a cloud,
To damp our brainless ardours, and abate
That glare of life which often blinds the wise:
Our dying friends are pioneers, to smooth
Our rugged pass to death; to break those bars
Of terror and abhorrence nature throws
Cross our obstructed way; and thus to make
Welcome as safe our port from every storm:
Each friend by fate snatch'd from us, is a plume

IV. pl. 27

55

Pluck'd from the wing of human vanity,
Which makes us stoop from our aërial heights,
And, damp'd with omen of our own decease,
On drooping pinions of ambition lower'd,
Just skim earth's surface, ere we break it up,
O'er putrid earth to scratch a little dust,
And save the world a nuisance: smitten friends
Are angels sent on errands full of love:
For us they languish, and for us they die:
And shall they languish, shall they die in vain?
* Ungrateful, shall we grieve their hovering shades
Which wait the revolution in our hearts?
Shall we disdain their silent soft address,
Their posthumous advice, and pious prayer?
Senseless as herds that graze their hallow'd graves,
Tread under foot their agonies and groans,
Frustrate their anguish, and destroy their deaths?
    LORENZO! no; the thought of death indulge;
Give it its wholesome empire—let it reign,
That kind chastiser of thy soul in joy;
Its reign will spread thy glorious conquests far,
And still the tumults of thy ruffled breast:
Auspicious æra! golden days, begin!
The thought of death shall, like a god, inspire.
And why not think on death? is life the theme
Of every thought? and wish of every hour?
And song of every joy? Surprising truth!
The beaten spaniel's fondness not so strange.
To wave the numerous ills that seize on life
As their own property, their lawful prey;

57

Still-streaming thoroughfares of dull debauch!
* Trembling each gulp, lest death should snatch the bowl.
 Such of our fine ones is the wish refined—
So would they have it: elegant desire!
Why not invite the bellowing stalls and wilds?
But such examples might their riot awe.
Through want of virtue, that is, want of thought,
Though on bright thought they father all their flights,
To what are they reduced? to love and hate
The same vain world; to censure and espouse
This painted shrew of life, who calls them fool
Each moment of each day; to flatter bad
Through dread of worse; to cling to this rude rock,
Barren, to them, of good, and sharp with ills,
And hourly blacken'd with impending storms,
And infamous for wrecks of human hope——
Scared at the gloomy gulph that yawns beneath.
Such are their triumphs! such their pangs of joy!
 'Tis time, high time to shift this dismal scene:
This hugg'd, this hideous state what art can cure?
One only, but that one what all may reach,
Virtue—she, wonder-working goddess! charms
That rock to bloom, and tames the painted shrew;
And what will more surprise, LORENZO! gives
To life's sick nauseous iteration, change;
And straitens nature's circle to a line.
Believest thou this, LORENZO? lend an ear,
A patient ear, thou'lt blush to disbelieve.
 A languid leaden iteration reigns,
And ever must, o'er those whose joys are joys

IV. pl. 29

63

To dust when drop proud nature's proudest spheres,
And live entire: death is the crown of life;
Were death denied, poor man would live in vain;
Were death denied, to live would not be life;
Were death denied, even fools would wish to die:
Death wounds to cure: we fall, we rise, we reign!
Spring from our fetters, fasten in the skies
Where blooming Eden withers in our sight.
Death gives us more than was in Eden lost;
*This KING OF TERRORS is the PRINCE OF PEACE.
When shall I die to vanity, pain, death?
When shall I die?—when shall I live for ever?

IV. pl. 30

IV. pl. 31

70

Caught at a court; purged off by purer air,
And simpler diet; gifts of rural life!
    Blest be that hand divine, which gently laid
My heart at rest, beneath this humble shed.
The world's a stately bark, on dangerous seas
With pleasure seen, but boarded at our peril:
Here, on a single plank thrown safe ashore,
I hear the tumult of the distant throng,
As that of seas remote, or dying storms;
And meditate on scenes more silent still;
Pursue my theme, and fight the fear of death.
Here, like a shepherd gazing from his hut,
Touching his reed or leaning on his staff,
Eager ambition's fiery chase I see;
I see the circling hunt of noisy men
Burst law's inclosure, leap the mounds of right,
Pursuing and pursued, each other's prey;
As wolves, for rapine; as the fox, for wiles;
* Till death, that mighty hunter, earths them all.
    Why all this toil for triumphs of an hour?
What, though we wade in wealth, or soar in fame,
Earth's highest station ends in, " here he lies!"
And " dust to dust" concludes her noblest song.
If this song live, posterity shall know
One, though in Britain born, with courtiers bred,
Who thought e'en gold might come a day too late;
Nor on his subtle death-bed plann'd his scheme
For future vacancies in church or state;
Some avocation deeming it———to die

IV. pl. 32

72

* And vapid; sense and reason shew the door,
Call for my bier, and point me to the dust.
 O THOU! great arbiter of life and death!
Nature's immortal, immaterial sun!
Whose all-prolific beam late call'd me forth
From darkness—teeming darkness where I lay
The worm's inferior, and in rank beneath
The dust I tread on, high to bear my brow,
To drink the spirit of the golden day,
And triumph in existence! and couldst know
No motive but my bliss! and hast ordain'd
A rise in blessing! with the patriarch's joy,
Thy call I follow to the land unknown:
I trust in THEE, and know in whom I trust:
Or life or death is equal; neither weighs;
All weight in this—O let me live to THEE!
 Though nature's terrors thus may be repress'd;
Still frowns grim death, guilt points the tyrant's spear:
And whence all human guilt?—from death forgot.
Ah me! too long I set at nought the swarm
Of friendly warnings which around me flew;
And smiled unsmitten: small my cause to smile!
Death's admonitions, like shafts upward shot,
More dreadful by delay; the longer ere
They strike our hearts, the deeper is their wound:
O think how deep, LORENZO! here it stings:
Who can appease its anguish? how it burns!
What hand the barb'd, envenom'd thought can draw?
What healing hand can pour the balm of peace,
And turn my sight undaunted on the tomb?

IV. pl. 33

73

With joy—with grief, that healing hand I see;
Ah! too conspicuous! it is fix'd on high!
On high?—what means my phrensy? I blaspheme;
Alas! how low! how far beneath the skies—
The skies it form'd! and now it bleeds for me:
But bleeds the balm I want?—yet still it bleeds.
* Draw the dire steel?—ah no!—the dreadful blessing
What heart or can sustain, or dares forego?
There hangs all human hope!!! that nail supports
The falling universe!!! that gone, we drop!
Horror receives us, and the dismal wish
Creation had been smother'd in her birth:
Darkness his curtain! and his bed the dust!
When stars and sun are dust beneath his throne:
In heaven itself can such indulgence dwell?
O what a groan was there! a groan not his,
HE seized our dreadful right; the load sustain'd;
And heaved the mountain from a guilty world:
A thousand worlds so bought were bought too dear.
Sensations new, in angels bosoms rise;
Suspend their song, and make a pause in bliss.
 O for their song to reach my lofty theme!
Inspire me, night! with all thy tuneful spheres inspire,
Whilst I with seraphs share seraphic themes,
And shew to men the dignity of man;
Lest I blaspheme my subject with my song.
Shall pagan pages glow celestial flame,
And christian languish? on our hearts, not heads,
Falls the foul infamy: my heart! awake;
What can awake thee, unawaked by this?—

IV. pl. 34

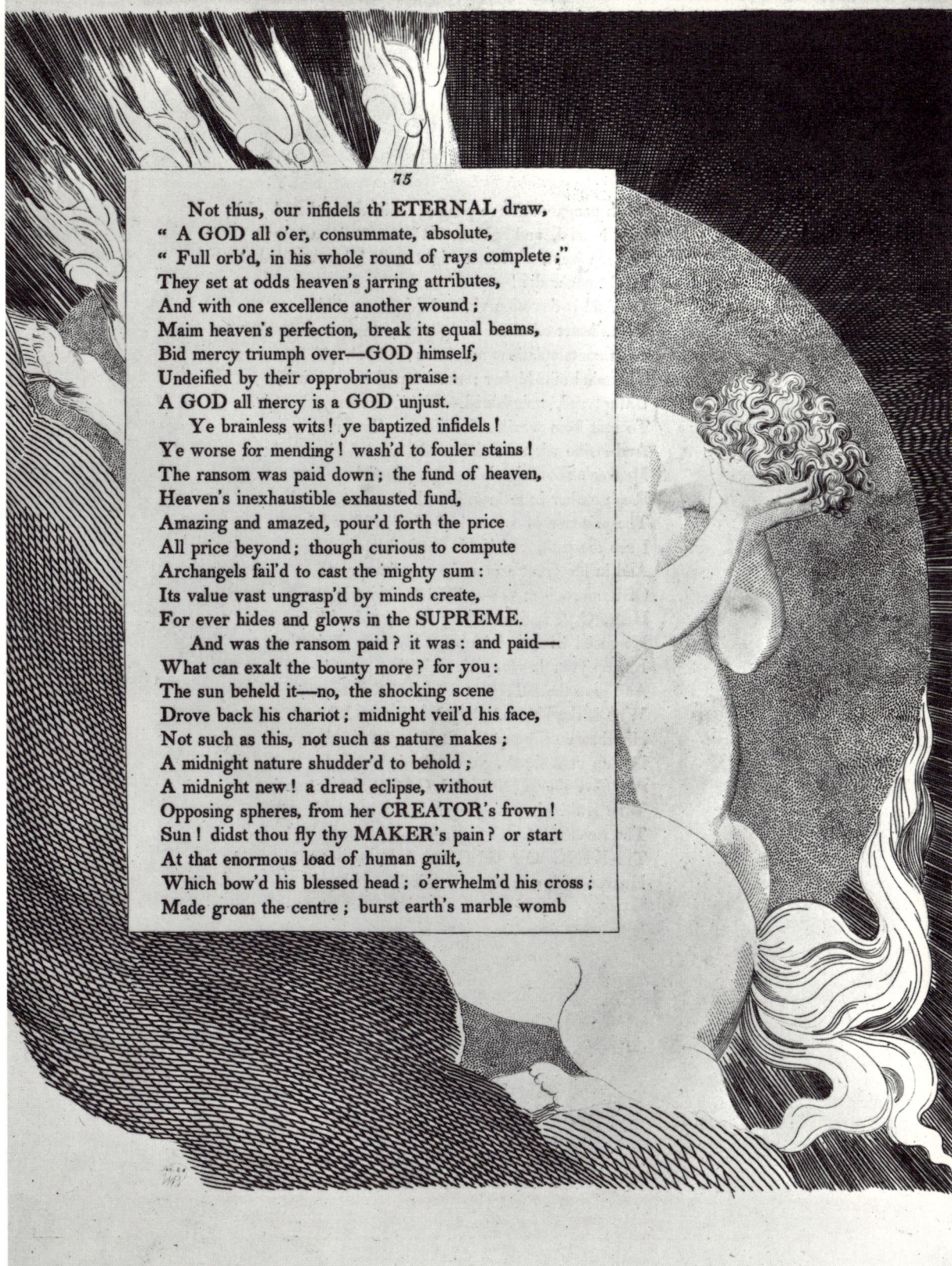

75

Not thus, our infidels th' ETERNAL draw,
" A GOD all o'er, consummate, absolute,
" Full orb'd, in his whole round of rays complete;"
They set at odds heaven's jarring attributes,
And with one excellence another wound;
Maim heaven's perfection, break its equal beams,
Bid mercy triumph over——GOD himself,
Undeified by their opprobrious praise:
A GOD all mercy is a GOD unjust.
    Ye brainless wits! ye baptized infidels!
Ye worse for mending! wash'd to fouler stains!
The ransom was paid down; the fund of heaven,
Heaven's inexhaustible exhausted fund,
Amazing and amazed, pour'd forth the price
All price beyond; though curious to compute
Archangels fail'd to cast the mighty sum:
Its value vast ungrasp'd by minds create,
For ever hides and glows in the SUPREME.
    And was the ransom paid? it was: and paid——
What can exalt the bounty more? for you:
The sun beheld it——no, the shocking scene
Drove back his chariot; midnight veil'd his face,
Not such as this, not such as nature makes;
A midnight nature shudder'd to behold;
A midnight new! a dread eclipse, without
Opposing spheres, from her CREATOR's frown!
Sun! didst thou fly thy MAKER's pain? or start
At that enormous load of human guilt,
Which bow'd his blessed head; o'erwhelm'd his cross;
Made groan the centre; burst earth's marble womb

IV. pl. 35

80

What, night eternal—but a frown from thee?
What, heaven's meridian glory—but thy smile?
And shall not praise be thine? not human praise?
While heaven's high host on hallelujahs live?
    O may I breathe no longer than I breathe
My soul in praise to HIM who gave my soul
And all her infinite of prospect fair;
Cut through the shades of hell, great love! by THEE,
Oh most adorable, most unadored!
Where shall that praise begin, which ne'er should end?
Where'er I turn, what claim on all applause!
How is night's sable mantle labour'd o'er!
How richly wrought with attributes divine!
What wisdom shines! what love! this midnight pomp,
This gorgeous arch with golden worlds inlaid,
Built with divine ambition, nought to THEE!
For others this profusion: THOU apart,
Above, beyond: oh tell me, mighty mind!
Where art thou? shall I dive into the deep?
Call to the sun, or ask the roaring winds
For their creator? shall I question loud
* The thunder, if in that the ALMIGHTY dwells?
Or holds HE furious storms in streighten'd reins,
And bids fierce whirlwinds wheel his rapid car?
    What mean these questions?—trembling I retract;
My prostrate soul adores the present GOD:
Praise I a distant DEITY? HE tunes
My voice, if tuned; the nerve that writes, sustains;
Wrapp'd in his being I resound his praise:
But though past all diffused, without a shore

IV. pl. 36

Supporter sole of man above himself;
Even in this night of frailty, change, and death,
She gives the soul a soul that acts a God.
Religion! providence! an after-state!
Here is firm footing—here is solid rock—
This can support us—all is sea besides—
Sinks under us—bestorms, and then devours.
* His hand the good man fastens on the skies,
And bids earth roll, nor feels her idle whirl.

    As when a wretch, from thick polluted air,
Darkness and stench, and suffocating damps,
And dungeon-horrors by kind fate discharged,
Climbs some fair eminence, where ether pure
Surrounds him, and elysian prospects rise;
His heart exults, his spirits cast their load;
As if new-born he triumphs in the change;
So joys the soul, when, from inglorious aims
And sordid sweets, from feculence and froth
Of ties terrestrial set at large, she mounts
To reason's region, her own element,
Breathes hopes immortal and affects the skies.

    Religion! thou the soul of happiness;
And, groaning Calvary, of thee! there shine
The noblest truths; there strongest motives sting;
There sacred violence assaults the soul;
There nothing but compulsion is forborn.
Can love allure us? or can terror awe?
HE weeps!—the falling drop puts out the sun;
HE sighs!—the sigh earth's deep foundation shakes:
If in his love so terrible, what then

IV. pl. 37

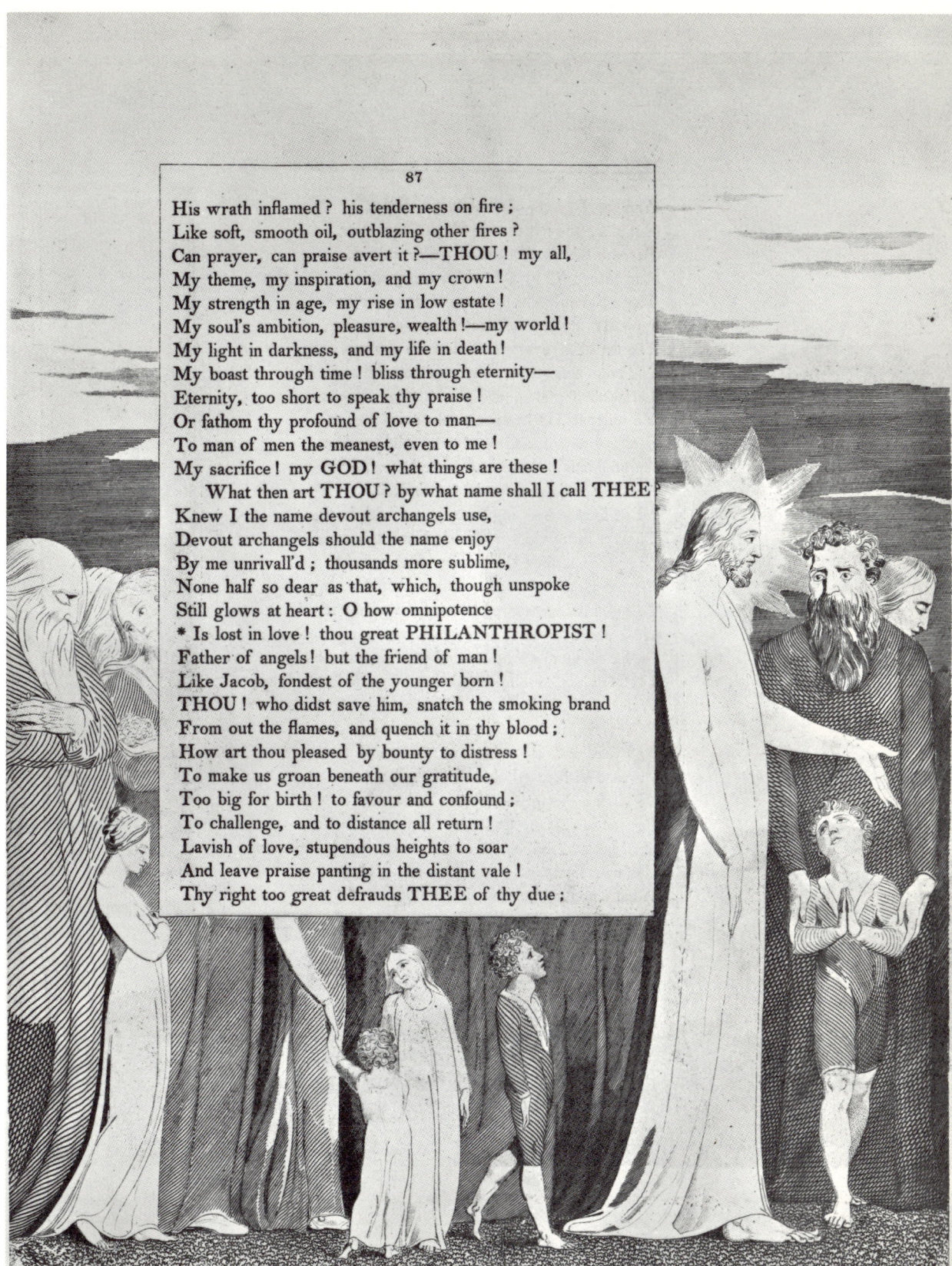

87

His wrath inflamed ? his tenderness on fire ;
Like soft, smooth oil, outblazing other fires ?
Can prayer, can praise avert it ?—THOU ! my all,
My theme, my inspiration, and my crown !
My strength in age, my rise in low estate !
My soul's ambition, pleasure, wealth !—my world !
My light in darkness, and my life in death !
My boast through time ! bliss through eternity—
Eternity, too short to speak thy praise !
Or fathom thy profound of love to man—
To man of men the meanest, even to me !
My sacrifice ! my GOD ! what things are these !
    What then art THOU ? by what name shall I call THEE
Knew I the name devout archangels use,
Devout archangels should the name enjoy
By me unrivall'd ; thousands more sublime,
None half so dear as that, which, though unspoke
Still glows at heart : O how omnipotence
* Is lost in love ! thou great PHILANTHROPIST !
Father of angels ! but the friend of man !
Like Jacob, fondest of the younger born !
THOU ! who didst save him, snatch the smoking brand
From out the flames, and quench it in thy blood ;
How art thou pleased by bounty to distress !
To make us groan beneath our gratitude,
Too big for birth ! to favour and confound ;
To challenge, and to distance all return !
Lavish of love, stupendous heights to soar
And leave praise panting in the distant vale !
Thy right too great defrauds THEE of thy due ;

IV. pl. 38

88

And sacrilegious our sublimest song:
But since the naked will obtains thy smile,
Beneath this monument of praise unpaid,
And future life symphonious to my strain,
That noblest hymn to heaven! for ever lie
Intomb'd my fear of death! and every fear,
The dread of every evil, but thy frown.
    Whom see I yonder, so demurely smile?
Laughter a labour, and might break their rest.
Ye quietists, in homage to the skies!
Serene! of soft address! who mildly make
An unobtrusive tender of your hearts,
Abhorring violence! who halt indeed,
* But for the blessing wrestle not with heaven!
Think you my song too turbulent? too warm?
Are passions then the pagans of the soul?
Reason alone baptized—alone ordain'd
To touch things sacred?—oh for warmer still!
Guilt chills my zeal, and age benumbs my powers;
Oh for an humbler heart, and prouder song!
THOU! my much-injured theme! with that soft eye
Which melted o'er doom'd Salem, deign to look
Compassion to the coldness of my breast;
And pardon to the winter in my strain!
Oh ye cold-hearted, frozen formalists!
On such a theme 'tis impious to be calm;
Passion is reason, transport temper, here.
Shall heaven, which gave us ardour, and has shewn
Her own for man so strongly, not disdain
What smooth emollients in theology,

IV. pl. 39

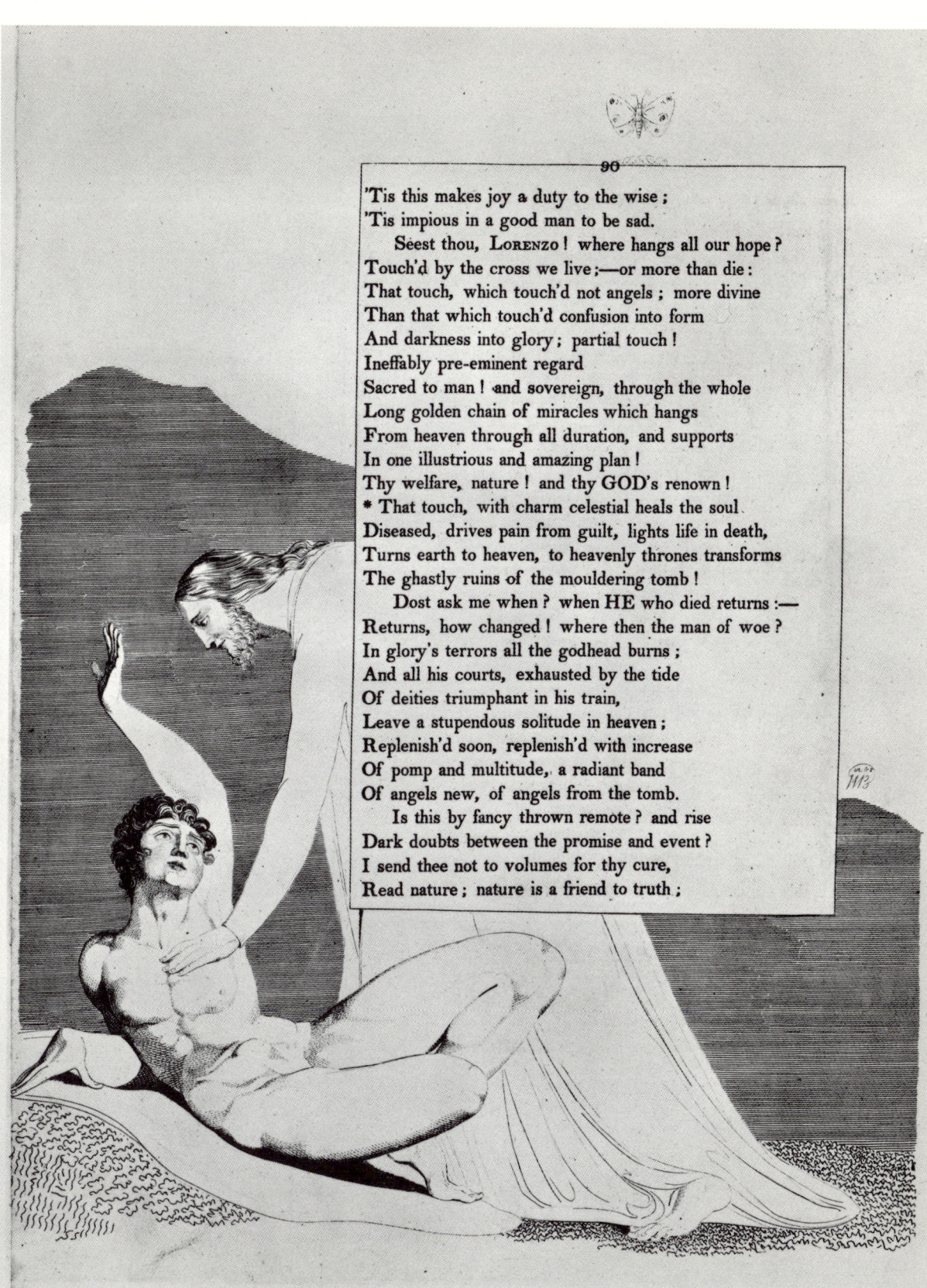

90

'Tis this makes joy a duty to the wise;
'Tis impious in a good man to be sad.
    Seest thou, LORENZO! where hangs all our hope?
Touch'd by the cross we live;—or more than die:
That touch, which touch'd not angels; more divine
Than that which touch'd confusion into form
And darkness into glory; partial touch!
Ineffably pre-eminent regard
Sacred to man! and sovereign, through the whole
Long golden chain of miracles which hangs
From heaven through all duration, and supports
In one illustrious and amazing plan!
Thy welfare, nature! and thy GOD's renown!
* That touch, with charm celestial heals the soul
Diseased, drives pain from guilt, lights life in death,
Turns earth to heaven, to heavenly thrones transforms
The ghastly ruins of the mouldering tomb!
    Dost ask me when? when HE who died returns:—
Returns, how changed! where then the man of woe?
In glory's terrors all the godhead burns;
And all his courts, exhausted by the tide
Of deities triumphant in his train,
Leave a stupendous solitude in heaven;
Replenish'd soon, replenish'd with increase
Of pomp and multitude, a radiant band
Of angels new, of angels from the tomb.
    Is this by fancy thrown remote? and rise
Dark doubts between the promise and event?
I send thee not to volumes for thy cure,
Read nature; nature is a friend to truth;

IV. pl. 40

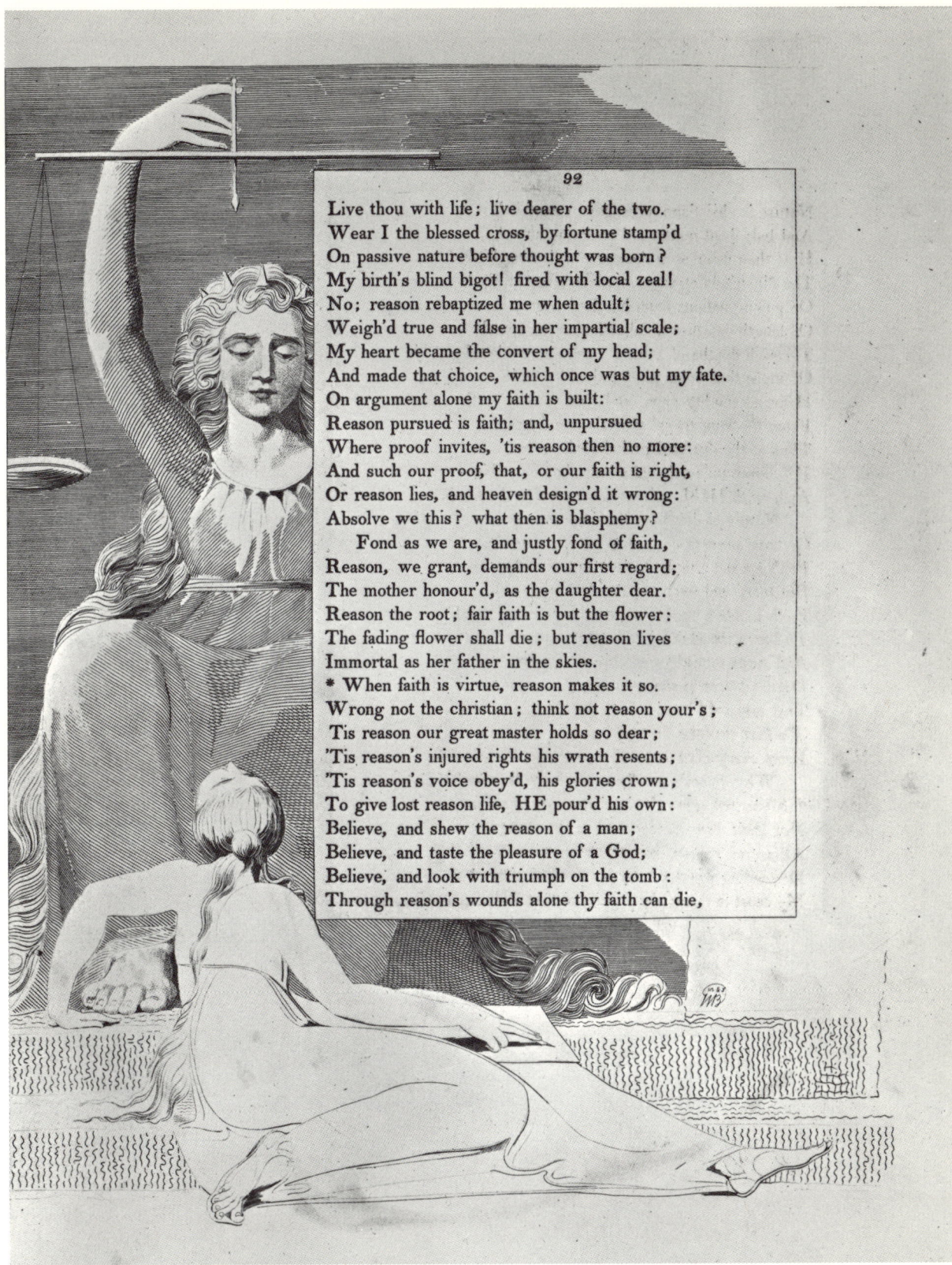

92

Live thou with life; live dearer of the two.
Wear I the blessed cross, by fortune stamp'd
On passive nature before thought was born?
My birth's blind bigot! fired with local zeal!
No; reason rebaptized me when adult;
Weigh'd true and false in her impartial scale;
My heart became the convert of my head;
And made that choice, which once was but my fate.
On argument alone my faith is built:
Reason pursued is faith; and, unpursued
Where proof invites, 'tis reason then no more:
And such our proof, that, or our faith is right,
Or reason lies, and heaven design'd it wrong:
Absolve we this? what then is blasphemy?

    Fond as we are, and justly fond of faith,
Reason, we grant, demands our first regard;
The mother honour'd, as the daughter dear.
Reason the root; fair faith is but the flower:
The fading flower shall die; but reason lives
Immortal as her father in the skies.
* When faith is virtue, reason makes it so.
Wrong not the christian; think not reason your's;
'Tis reason our great master holds so dear;
'Tis reason's injured rights his wrath resents;
'Tis reason's voice obey'd, his glories crown;
To give lost reason life, HE pour'd his own:
Believe, and shew the reason of a man;
Believe, and taste the pleasure of a God;
Believe, and look with triumph on the tomb:
Through reason's wounds alone thy faith can die,

IV. pl. 41

IV. pl. 42

95

By the great edict, the divine decree,
Truth is deposited with man's last hour;
An honest hour, and faithful to her trust:
Truth, eldest daughter of the Deity;
Truth, of his council when he made the worlds,
Nor less when he shall judge the worlds he made;
Though silent long, and sleeping ne'er so sound
Smother'd with errors, and oppress'd with toys;
That heaven-commission'd hour no sooner calls,
But from her cavern in the soul's abyss,
Like him they fable under Ætna whelm'd,
* The goddess bursts in thunder and in flame;
Loudly convinces, and severely pains:
Dark demons I discharge, and hydra-stings;
The keen vibration of bright truth—is hell:
Just definition! though by schools untaught.
Ye deaf to truth! peruse this parson'd page,
And trust for once a prophet and a priest;
" Men may live fools, but fools they cannot die."

IV. pl. 43

Little TOM the Sailor

And does then the Ocean possess
The promising, brave, little youth,
Who display'd, in a scene of distress,
Such Tenderness, Courage, and Truth?

Little Tom is a Cottagers Son;
His years not amounting to ten;
But the Dawn of his Manhood begun
With a Soul like the noblest of Men.

In an Hospital, distant from Home,
He lost his unfortunate Sire;
And his Mother was tempted to roam,
But to see that kind Father expire.

To depart from her Cottage was hard;
To desert the dear dying was worse.
Tho'! She had an Ideot to guard,
And a sick little Infant to nurse.

The brave little Tom tried to chear
The Grief that He shudder'd to see:
"Go! Mother (He said) without Fear!
Go! and leave these poor Creatures to me!

Go, you my sick Father restore!
And I will take Care of these two;
I will not stir out of the Door,
For what without me could they do?

I will carefully dress them, and feed,
Go you our dear Father to save!
I will not desert them indeed:"
And Tom kept the promise he gave.

V. William Hayley, *Little Tom the Sailor*, pl. 1 and upper part of pl. 2

But his Mother a Widow came back,
Want, and Sorrow her Portion must be;
And her Heart, on Necessity's Rack,
Has sent little Thomas to Sea.

O Sea! Thou grand Servant of God!
The Children of Britain defend!
As a braver the Deck never trod,
Little Thomas will find Thee a Friend.

And when He's aloft in the Shrouds,
If a Storm threats aloud, to destroy,
His Fathers free Soul, in the Clouds,
Will watch o'er the venturous Boy:

I hear, when the Tempests appall,
That Spirit paternal exclaim:—
"O God! Thou Protector of All!
Let me shelter this dear little Frame!

A Defender, with Honour, his Due!
In the Man, may his Country admire!
Since the Child was a Guardian so true
To the desolate Cot of his Sire."

Printed for & Sold by the Widow Spicer of Folkstone
for the Benefit of her Orphans
October 5, 1800

V. Lower part of pl. 2 and pls. 3 and 4

VI. William Hayley, *Designs to a Series of Ballads.* pl. 1

VI. pl. 2

VI. pl. 3

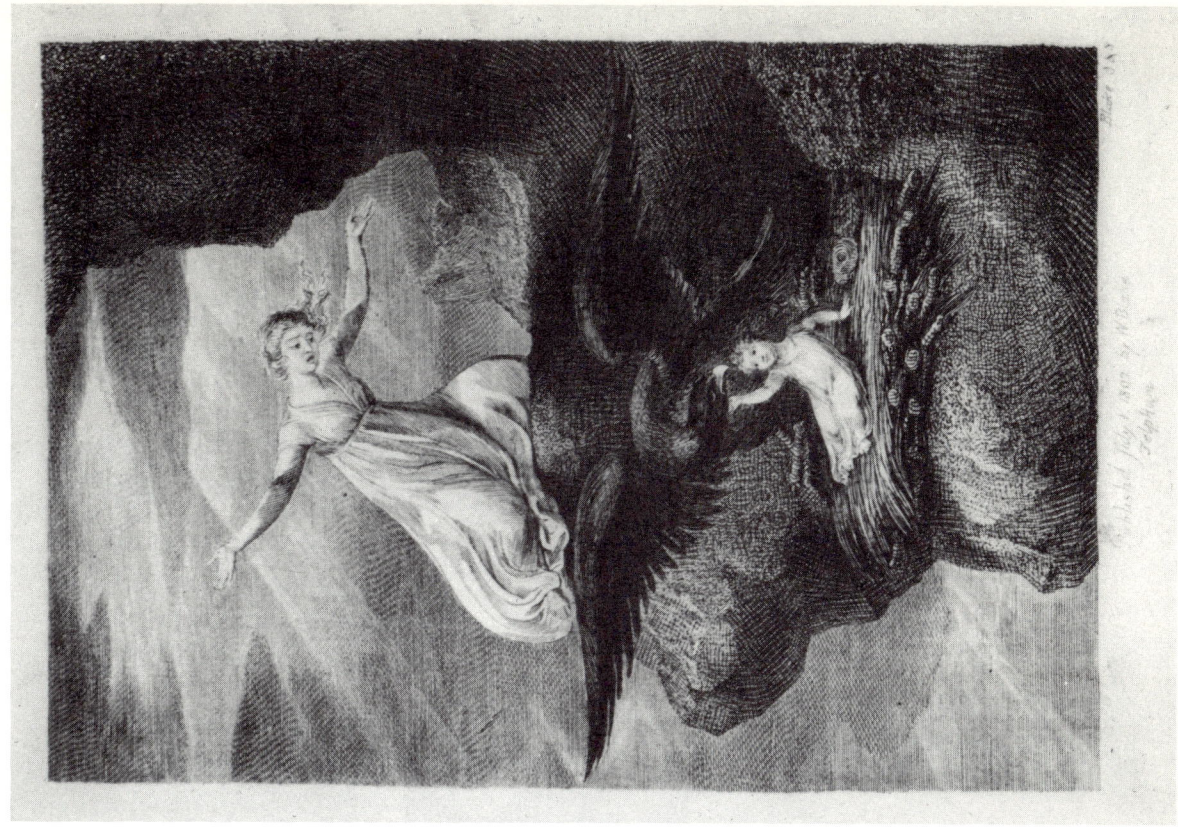

VI. pl. 5

VI. pl. 4

VI. pl. 6

VI. pl. 7

VI. pl. 9

VI. pl. 8

VI. pl. 10

VI. pl. 12

VI. pl. 11

VII. William Hayley, *The Life and Posthumous Writings of William Cowper*. pl. 1A

VIII. pl. 2A

VIII. William Hayley, *Ballads* (1805). pl. 1A

VIII. pl. 4

VIII. pl. 3A

IX. The Prologue and Characters of Chaucer's Pilgrims. pl. 1

IX. pl. 2

VIII. pl. 5

X. Robert John Thornton, *The Pastorals of Virgil*.
Proof Sheet of Nos. 8-11 before the woodblocks
were cut down for publication

To face page 15.
ILLUSTRATIONS OF IMITATION OF ECLOGUE I.

THENOT.

THENOT.

COLINET.

COLINET.

X. nos. 6-9

To face page 14.
ILLUSTRATIONS OF IMITATION OF ECLOGUE I.

COLINET.

THENOT.

COLINET and THENOT.

COLINET.

X. nos. 2-5

To face page 13

ILLUSTRATIONS OF IMITATION OF ECLOGUE I.

Thenot. To illustrate lines 1, 2.

3, 4, 5, 6.

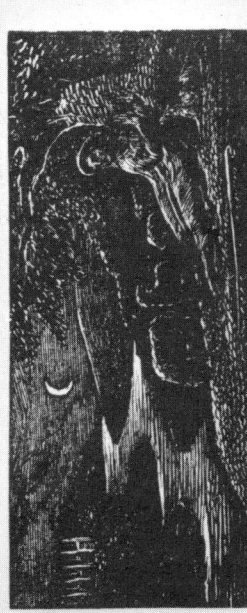

7, 8, 9.

10.

X. nos. 14-17

To face page 15.

ILLUSTRATIONS OF IMITATION OF ECLOGUE I.

THENOT.

COLINET.

COLINET.

THENOT.

X. nos. 10-13

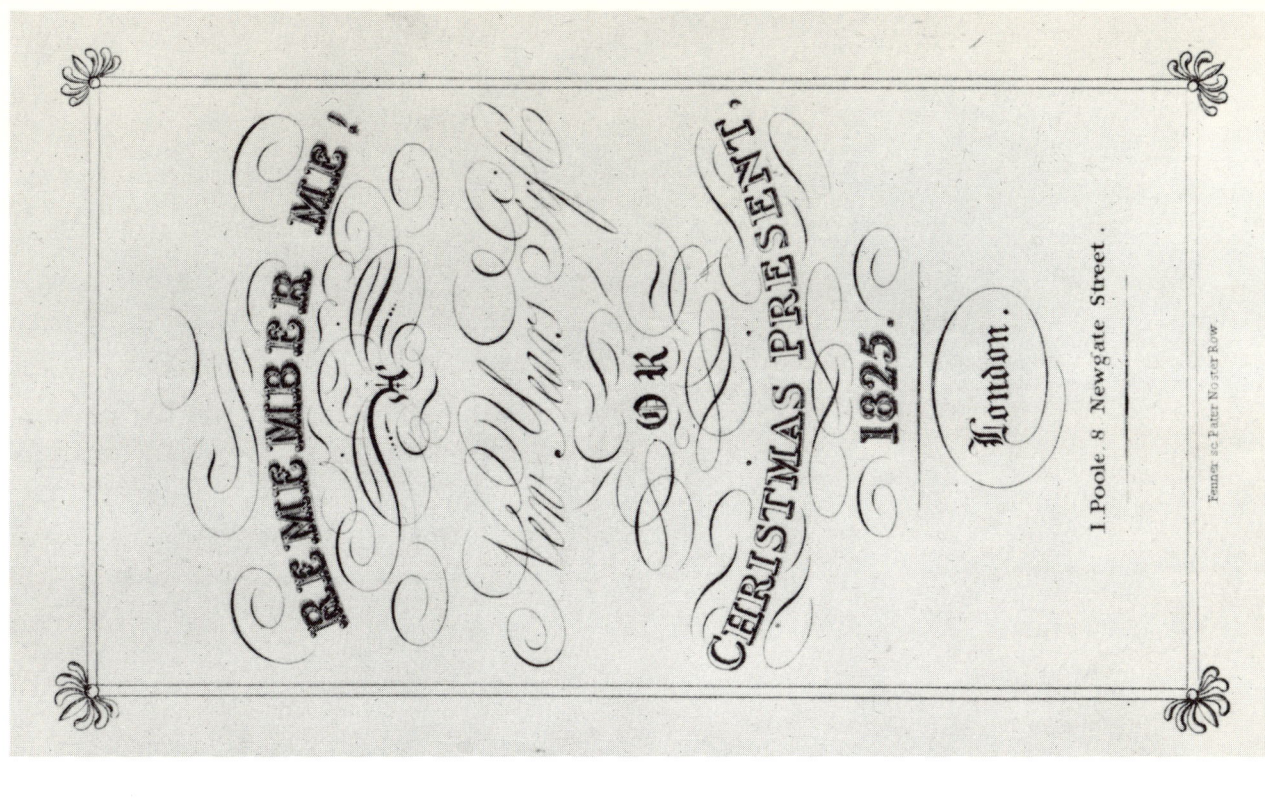

XI. *Remember Me!*, engraved title page, first edition. pl. 2 [Plate enlarged]

XI. *Remember Me!* pl. 1